W9-CKH-215

the

Co-Dependent
PARENT

Also by Barbara Cottman Becnel:

Parents Who Help Their Children Overcome Drugs

the

Co-Dependent
Parent

BARBARA
COTTMAN
BECNEL

Free Yourself by

Freeing Your Child

Lowell House
Los Angeles
Contemporary Books
Chicago

Library of Congress Cataloging-in-Publication Data

Becnel, Barbara Cottman.
    The co-dependent parent : free yourself by freeing
your child/Barbara Cottman Becnel.
        p. cm.
    Includes bibliographical references.
    ISBN 0-929923-12-X
    1. Parent and child–United States.   2. Co-
    dependence (Psychology)   3. Problem families–
    United States. 4. Parenting–United States.
    I. Title.
    HQ755.85.B435   1990
    306.874–dc20   90-5478
                                                            CIP

Copyright © 1990 by RGA Publishing Group, Inc., and
Barbara Cottman Becnel

All rights reserved. No part of this work may be
reproduced or transmitted in any form or by any means,
electronic or mechanical, including photocopying and
recording, or by any information storage or retrieval
system, except as may be expressly permitted by the 1976
Copyright Act or in writing by the publisher.

Requests for such permissions should be addressed to:

LOWELL HOUSE
1875 Century Park East, Suite 220
Los Angeles, CA 90067

Publisher: JACK ARTENSTEIN
Vice President/Editor-in-Chief: JANICE GALLAGHER
Marketing Manager: ELIZABETH WOOD
Design: MIKE YAZZOLINO

Manufactured in the United States of America

10   9   8   7   6   5   4   3   2   1

This book is for my mother, whom I have finally
come to know and love as myself.

ACKNOWLEDGMENTS

I am most grateful for the opportunity to work again with such a talented and supportive editor, Janice Gallagher. My publisher, Jack Artenstein, also deserves the heartiest of thank-you's for his ongoing faith in my work. I am particularly appreciative of my loving husband, who nurtured me through the sometimes torturous process of writing a book. He also spent many a late night reading my material, which resulted in his providing invaluable insight and assistance that improved the quality of my manuscript.

A special thank-you is in order for my good friend Lisa Smith, who, by demonstrating the courage to heal herself, assisted in the development of this book's recovery program. Also, I am most grateful for the participation of all of the families who consented to be interviewed for this book. Their openness was extraordinary.

Finally, I want to thank my mother for being my mother, a role model I have come to truly appreciate.

CONTENTS

INTRODUCTION:
AND THE HEALING BEGINS...

Chances are we have a lot in common.

As a child, I often lied to protect my father, a compulsive gambler, when loan sharks banged on our door. As a child, I became an over-achiever in my attempt to meet the unattainable standards my mother established. As an adult, I became a super-ambitious workaholic in an unconscious effort to gain her approval.

I also took on the role of family hero and became my younger sister's surrogate mom whenever she had a falling-out with our mother. During such periods, I allowed my sister to live with me, bought her clothes, and helped pay for her short-lived college education.

I also used my workaholism to avoid accepting the responsibility for raising my son. I retreated from the rigors and routine of parenthood and became a disengaging mother who simply wasn't around very much to nurture my child. To relieve my guilt about not being a "traditional" parent, I became a compulsive spender in an attempt to buy my son's love.

Though the details of my history may differ from your experiences, the unhealthy quality that characterized my life is probably not appreciably different from yours. I behaved as I did because of what I learned from my parents. Likewise, their behavior was a reflection of how *they* were raised. In other words, I was a co-dependent victim of two victims of co-dependency. And we all behaved in ways that unwittingly maintained one another's low self-esteem.

In preparing this book, I interviewed numerous parents across the United States. These families speak for themselves in the family profiles in Chapters 3 through 7. I spoke to as many members of these families as were willing or able to participate in this project. I did not alter their testimony; I simply reported what I heard. Given that approach, you may notice some inconsistencies, since not all family members perceived specific incidents—or themselves, or each other—the same way. Also, each of these families and each family member is at a different stage in recovery. So I suggest that you let the entire story unfold before you assess what "really" happened with these mothers, fathers, daughters, and sons, and then work through the exercise at the end of each profile. Even if an exercise does not appear to apply to your circumstance, do it anyway. Such efforts will play an important role in your recovery process, described in Chapter 9's Four-Phase Healing Program.

This book is designed to help both you and your child. The truth is, *your freedom from co-dependency is tied to your capacity to assist your child in freeing himself or herself from similar co-dependent patterns.*

The purpose of *The Co-Dependent Parent,* therefore, is to help parents and children overcome denial about their co-dependency, to help parents realize that they are not alone, to demonstrate that recovery is possible and that both parent and child can reap rewards as soon as the recovery process begins.

Beyond that, you will learn—as I did with some relief—that recovery is not a mysterious activity. In fact, all it requires is that you are willing to do a few simple yet extraordinary things: summon the courage to acknowledge and accept your co-dependent legacy, and develop new patterns of healthy behavior that you can practice throughout your lifetime.

PART 1

A PROFILE OF CO-DEPENDENT PARENTING

Most of us are co-dependent parents to a greater or lesser degree. That is so because our mothers and fathers are the most important role models we will ever have, and, to some degree, our parents were also co-dependent. Part One, therefore, asks you to consider the possibility that you are a co-dependent parent.

You will be helped to recognize even subtle symptoms of co-dependency in yourself, your spouse, and your son or daughter. Chapter 1 looks at the perils of what is often thought to be "good" parenting, and explains the difference between good parenting and responsible parenting. In addition, it examines the "co-" phenomenon of co-dependency to help parents understand how a co-dependent legacy is perpetuated.

Chapter 2 reveals the subtle dynamics of co-dependent family life by looking at four primary roles into which children from co-dependent families are typically cast—the hero, the scapegoat, the lost child, and the mascot.

It always takes at least two to engage in co-dependent patterns of behavior. Both you and your child, then, may be playing an unintentionally unhealthy game that requires each other's participation.

CHAPTER 1

PARENTS–
OUR QUINTESSENTIAL TEACHERS

Just about everything I've learned that did not come from a book I was taught by my parents. Some of what I learned I absorbed voluntarily, and I was happy to have been the recipient of the knowledge. Certain other "messages" from my mother and father were harder to swallow. I rejected some of them out of hand and gave them no further thought; other parental entreaties set in motion a lifelong rebellion. For years, then, I thought everything I had picked up from my mom and dad had been consciously transmitted by them to me. I also gave myself credit for deliberately embracing or rejecting their wisdom. As I got older, though, I noticed something that was at first shocking: in many ways I behaved just like Mother and Father, and I did not always find this behavior attractive.

In fact, I discovered that my parents and I shared the same unhealthy co-dependent behavioral patterns. Our co-dependency was displayed primarily in our insecurity—we needed to be needed in order to feel good about ourselves—which is the fundamental definition of co-dependency. So, I raised my son in ways that made him dependent on me to ensure his neediness, which, in turn, fed *my* neediness. As long as he couldn't break away from me I was content, though I claimed the contrary to anyone who would listen. My parents had followed a similar pattern.

I was most alarmed by this revelation because I couldn't pinpoint how the character exchange had taken place. Each day I wondered what else might be revealed about the connection between my habits and those of my parents. These discoveries were all the more discomforting because it was clear that Mother and Father had not intended to teach me things that worked against my good health and well-being. I know they saw themselves as good parents. Yet, as an adult, I was emulating not only the best but also, in more ways than I wanted to admit, the worst of my parents' behavior.

On the face of it, my upbringing was conventional. I was raised in a middle-class environment. My father drove a truck for the U.S. Post Office, and Mother was a schoolteacher. My younger sister, brother, and I ate well, dressed well, and lived in a house in a nice section of Philadelphia. Our family life was dysfunctional, however, for many reasons, some of which were more obvious than others.

Father's relationship with us children was starkly different from his relationship with our mother. To the kids he was kind and patient and could be counted on to purchase the impractical gifts Mother wouldn't think to buy. Yet he drank a lot and was a wife-beater and a compulsive gambler who borrowed money from loan sharks to cover his losses. These loan sharks didn't check credit references, but they did charge very high interest rates and required that the money be repaid quickly. When Father couldn't pay his debts, "collectors" were dispatched to bang on our front door at all hours of the day and night. Such shadowy figures scared me, but I was often the one who confronted these characters, having been instructed by Father to lie about his whereabouts. I felt I owed him allegiance, so I followed his instructions to give him more time to raise the money he owed.

Mother, on the other hand, was the essence of respectability and re- sponsibility. Sometimes she worked two jobs, teaching during the day and evening, to make up for the financial losses caused by Father's gam- bling. She also controlled the family in other ways. It was Mother who signed our report cards and visited our teachers. It was Mother who de- cided when my sister and I could wear lipstick, nylon stockings, and go on dates. She determined when my brother could get his driver's license and how long he was allowed to stay out when using the family car. Mother also was the disciplinarian. Any and all decisions of import had to be cleared through her. Father had very little voice in running our fami- ly's affairs. Mother ruled the household.

Years later, as I undertook the writing of this book, I interviewed my son, a 22-year-old, who helped me recognize the similarities between my parents, my first husband (his father), and myself. What I discovered was that I had unwittingly patterned my adult relationships after the way my mother and father interacted with each other. Indeed, my parents had proven to be my most important role models, my quintessential teachers.

A role model teaches by example rather than by providing clearly articulated instructions. So, while some of what I learned from my parents was obvious, other behaviors were conveyed very subtly. When I lied to loan sharks at my father's request, for example, a number of obvious and not-so-obvious messages were transmitted to me. One message was inconsistency. I had been taught over the years to be an honest person. But during my encounters with loan sharks I learned that telling the truth wasn't always the most desirable course of action, especially with regard to my parents' affairs. A more subtle message centered on whether I should trust a person's kind deeds, since I felt my father exacted dishonesty from me as repayment for the impractical gifts he regularly bestowed upon his children. In essence, I learned that presents often come with strings attached. It frightened me, too, that he might withdraw his love if I didn't comply with his wishes. If I displayed any resistance, Father would immediately frown, become stoic, and refuse to communicate. The net effect was that I instantly became an outcast in my own home.

What I learned from the model of resilience my mother provided was that it was important to be a survivor, to stay and struggle with very unhealthy situations even if they lasted 25 years, as did my parents' marriage. I also learned—from my mother's decision to work two jobs in order to maintain our middle-class status—that nice clothes and a well-appointed home should be favored over allowing the time to provide nurturing. With that observation in mind, I determined that workaholism must be a good thing. Later, I acted out well what I was "taught" by both parents, as the dynamics of my first marriage aptly demonstrate.

Shortly after we were married, my husband, a college student, became impatient with how much money he could earn legitimately and began instead to work hard to make "big" money quickly—and, for the most part, illegally. He also used drugs, and during arguments he beat me. For a while, though I was depressed about the way I was living, I did not leave. Indeed, on some levels I involved myself in his lifestyle. Often, for instance, I lied to my husband's unsavory associates to "protect" him, just as I lied to family and friends about the misery of my day-to-day existence in an attempt to protect the middle-class image of myself I wanted to project. I worked as a civil servant while my husband accumulated a large cash reserve of ill-gotten gains. It took a couple of years and several aborted attempts to leave before I mustered up the courage to divorce him and thus give up my unacknowledged belief that I should stand by him and be a survivor—no matter at what cost.

Through interviewing my son for this book about how he was raised, I was prompted to take another look at my past. What I learned was unnerving: in many ways I chose the same type of man my mother chose to marry and, for the most part, I was the same type of wife she had been. I also learned that we were all co-dependent parents.

THE "GOOD" PARENT

You are likely reading *The Co-Dependent Parent* because you want to stay abreast of whatever information is available to help you raise healthy, well-adjusted children. You probably consider yourself a good parent. You work hard and try hard, because you want to do the very best for your children. You may not understand, however, what being a good parent really means. The definition is not as clear-cut as it may seem. More likely than not, what you see as being good parenting is really co-dependent parenting. In fact, the five primary beliefs that underlie what most adults consider to be good parenting often are symptoms of co-dependency:

1. I must control my children.
2. I am superior to my children.
3. My children owe me for what I do for them.
4. I must be a perfect parent.
5. My children are more important than I am.

Each of these co-dependent beliefs has a healthy counterpart in the model of behavior for truly responsible parents. However, it's easy to confuse what is normally considered "good" parenting (read "co-dependent" parenting) and responsible parenting. Some of the distinctions are very subtle, which accounts for why so many of us parents have been slow to diagnose our behavior as co-dependency. Taking heed of these distinctions, however, is critical in preparing your child for a successful transition to adulthood.

Since most of us are co-dependent parents to some degree, don't be surprised or alarmed if you recognize yourself in one or more of the following examples. Having the courage to identify your co-dependent symptoms is the first step in your recovery, and the first step toward helping you begin to raise your child as a healthy, responsible human being: a truly strong, free person.

I Must Control My Children

Many mothers and fathers who consider themselves the best of parents insist on having ironclad control over their children. Given the challenges of today's environment—easy availability of drugs and the prevalence of gangs in urban areas—it's understandable that parents would want to stay on top of their child's every movement. *Demanding* control over others, however, is a classic symptom of co-dependency and leads to some very unhealthy results for both the child and parent.

This is a co-dependent category with which I am quite familiar. As a parent I often handed down edicts with little explanation and insisted that my son obey. I believed this was good parenting because I felt that as a female head of household I needed to be tough to control my son. I also had the strong conviction that any decision I made was the correct one and thus should not be challenged—especially by a child. My son's adaptation to my co-dependent parenting was to suppress his anger toward me and to keep me from knowing what was really going on inside him. Occasionally, though, he would punch his fist through a wall or a dresser, attributing his action to some minor frustration. When such explosions occurred I was always puzzled.

Underneath it all, parents who believe they must control their offspring are parents who want to make themselves right and their children wrong. These are parents who want to win at every turn. There are a number of unhealthy or dysfunctional consequences for the child who is raised by a controlling parent. One possible outcome is that the child rebels. A rebellious child wages a continuing war against his parents, wants to win every round of the battle, and feels he is right.

Another possible outcome is that the child will do as my son did in response to my controlling behavior: hide his true feelings. Such a child is likely to feel anxious and may want to seek revenge. (The first time my son punched an object, it was my favorite antique dresser, which remains cracked to this day.) Some children react as my sister did to my mother's insistence on controlling the household: they give up and feel that life is unfair. These children believe they have no control over their lives. Dominated by that belief, my sister became a drug abuser and in other ways demonstrated a lack of self-discipline. Other possible symptoms are the tendencies to evade responsibility, to lie, and to steal.

In contrast to the good parent's desire to control, mothers and fathers who follow the responsible parent model believe that their children can make many of their own decisions and *should* make as many of those decisions as maturity allows. Responsible parents encourage choices so that their offspring can begin to develop problem-solving skills. Children raised by this type of parent gain self-confidence and are eager to contribute and to accept responsibility. These children become resourceful people.

I Am Superior to My Children

Mothers and fathers who feel superior to their children typically act out that behavior in very subtle ways. These are parents who covertly dominate, and thus control, the lives of their children. Parents who need to feel they are superior generally lavish their children with gifts and opportunities to do things that are beyond the wildest dreams of most other children. Such parents want their children to have more than they had as children. On the face of it, that's a pretty noble motivator, and it's easy to see why parents fall into the trap of believing such behavior makes them good mothers and fathers. Problems arise because there is another, less visible, motivator at work: Superior parents overprotect and spoil their children because they really want to control their kids' lives. These parents place their children in an inferior position by leaving them ill-equipped to fend for themselves, depriving them of developing skills to acquire anything on their own.

One Los Angeles mother I spoke to who falls into this category completely supports her 20-year-old daughter, even though the daughter is employed and lives on her own. This parent had her daughter's new apartment completely remodeled and has made it her responsibility to keep it clean; she bought her daughter a car and pays the auto insurance; she purchases her daughter's clothes, and supplies her with vacations to places as far away as Hawaii. As a result, the daughter has developed virtually all of the possible unhealthy outcomes of being raised by a parent who feels superior to her child. Because she tries to spend as much on herself as her mother does, and also buys too many expensive presents for her close friends, this young woman has accumulated enormous credit card debts. On the other hand, she feels life is unfair and pities herself when others won't give to her the way her mother gives. She is rarely willing to take responsibility for her actions; she blames others instead.

Mothers and fathers who have learned how to become responsible parents reject the superior parenting model in favor of helping their children develop self-reliance by exhibiting a belief in the child's competency. These parents believe they are no more and no less worthwhile than their offspring; consequently, their children grow up believing in their own equality and the equality of others. Such parents also believe it's important to show their children respect by encouraging independence and by expecting the children to contribute to the efficiency of family operations—by doing chores, for example. Responsible parents expect their adult children to stand on their own two feet. The following excerpts from a memo published in the "Dear Abby" column of the *Los Angeles Times* on August 4, 1989, illustrate this point:

TO: Jeannine, Greg, Michelle and Renee
FROM: Mom and Dad
SUBJECT: Money

Since the subject of loaning money has come up from at least half of you this week, we decided we would let you know our feelings about this.

We will not loan any of you money except in the case of a bona fide emergency (severe illness, accident, etc.). Each of you has been blessed with intelligence, good health and the ability to earn a living. What you choose to do with your time and money is up to you....This probably puts us somewhere between minus 10 and zero on your popularity scale, but we feel this is the best thing for our family. We love each of you dearly and want to do for you what we think will benefit you most in your lifetime.

My Children Owe Me

Some parents, who consider themselves good parents, believe it's okay to demand excessive time, money, and devotion from their children because they are the sole providers for their offspring—because they are the parents, pure and simple. It's not too difficult to understand why parents might feel this way. Raising a child is a major investment of time, money, and emotion. A parent can expect to spend thousands of dollars and countless hours helping the child develop her full potential. In virtually any other type of relationship that involved the expenditure of as much cash and energy, a cost-benefit analysis certainly would be undertaken before a dollar was spent or a tear shed. With children, of course, calculations of that sort don't apply. Still, parents are human, and when we work hard for our children we are prone to want them to return the favor, or at least acknowledge the effort.

We fail our children, though, when we adopt the attitude that they owe us for what we do as parents. In this way, we teach our offspring that what we give comes with undeclared strings attached. Because they feel exploited by their parents, children from such households learn not to trust anyone—and they learn to exploit others.

My father, for instance, often told us kids there was only one thing he wanted from us: respect. Such a comment was always followed quickly by: "But I feel every parent is *entitled* to respect no matter what." In practice, what he said translated into this: As long as we were taken care of, he expected respect from his children no matter how he behaved toward us. Frequently I felt guilty if I didn't meet his demands when he felt I owed him something. Father saw this approach to parenting as a way of instilling solid values in his children and thus being a good parent. However, his belief actually worked against the best interests of his children. The message we got was that respect did not have to be earned and was one-sided: We had to respect our father; he did not have to respect us.

Mutual respect is the guiding principle of mothers and fathers who subscribe to the reponsible parenting model of behavior. These parents promote equality among their children and avoid creating situations and conflicts that might lead to their offspring feeling guilty. Children from these families freely respect their parents and themselves. They are generally more social than their youthful counterparts who are members of families where "debts" must be repaid by the child on a regular basis. These children tend to be more social because they are more trusting and less manipulative of others. Not surprisingly, more people like them.

I Must Be a Perfect Parent

Some mothers and fathers believe that a good parent is a "perfect" parent. Such parents want to provide the best possible role model for their children, which is admirable. Yet, there are huge potential pitfalls in trying to accomplish the impossible. First, we are all human, and, by definition, imperfect. Therefore, the parent who is striving for perfection is an unhappy person who has placed herself in a lose-lose situation: no matter how hard she tries, she cannot attain perfection. In addition, perfect parents tend to make those around them unhappy because they often demand perfection from their children as well as themselves. These are the parents who push their children to win Little League games, whether or not the kids show athletic talent, and who push them to earn straight A's in school, whether or not the children are capable of producing such a report card. Often these parents are very concerned about what others think, and always they are hypercritical, finding fault with their children and most anyone with whom they come in contact.

I, too, have suffered from the malady of wanting to be a perfect parent and thus have spent much of my life being critical of my child's imperfections. Recently I got my comeuppance when I was finding fault with mistakes my son had made and he abruptly asked: "When you were my age, didn't you make a lot of the same mistakes?"

Children who are raised by perfect parents tend to grow up feeling that they are never good enough. They generally worry about the opinions of others and work as hard at becoming perfect as their parents did. These are children who spend a lot of time discouraged, feeling like failures. I really resonate with this description. I have spent much of my life depressed because I believed I didn't measure up. Despite my many accomplishments, which include graduating from college in 2½ years, summa cum laude, I still felt that nothing I achieved was good enough. I always felt I should have done better, I could have done more.

Mothers and fathers who practice more healthy parenting accept that they are human and, by so doing, dare to be imperfect. These parents set realistic standards for themselves and for their children. They focus on their strengths and on their children's strengths. They are patient and less concerned with image than are parents who strive to create a perfect (co-dependent) household. Children raised in this healthier environment learn to focus on the task at hand, instead of fearing or anticipating failure, or second-guessing their every move. They tend to view mistakes as a challenge to keep trying until they get it right. These youth have the courage to try new experiences, and they are considerably more tolerant of others.

My Children Are More Important Than I Am

Not long ago a friend called me, very upset. He wanted some feedback on something his wife had just done. Their 21-year-old son, who had lost his driver's license because of drunk driving, wanted to attend a meeting across town for which he was now late. Earlier, his sisters had waited to take him with them to the meeting, but he had decided to visit his girlfriend instead. Now he was home and demanding that his mother drive him to the meeting. She was tired and didn't feel like making the drive, her husband didn't want her to make the drive, but eventually her son browbeat her into doing what he wanted. I have spoken to this mother on more than one occasion, so I know her parenting philosophy: she believes that a good parent should meet virtually every need or demand of her child. "After all," she reports, "they didn't ask to come here, so as parents we should do every single thing we can for them." This is a co-dependent parent who earnestly believes that her children are more important than she.

This idea permeates our culture. We've all heard tales about mothers who went hungry to feed their children, and about parents who have drowned so that their children might live. So it's no wonder this mother feels the way she does. Becoming a slave to your child, though, trains your child to disrespect the rights of others. Parents who feel guilty about saying no to a child are teaching their children that it's okay to be self-centered. When parents overindulge the child and give in to every whim, the child learns to expect the same treatment from others. But that rarely happens in life, which will lead to the child having poor social relationships. In addition, such children are likely to get into trouble with the law, since they have little respect for authority and expect immediate gratification.

Children raised in families run by responsible parents have good social relationships because their parents teach them that all people are important, including parents. These children show their parents respect, and the parents reciprocate. Responsible parents refuse to be doormats for their children. They know when to say no, and won't hesitate to do so. Their children expect to contribute to the well-being of the family rather than to foment dissension. Responsible parents, then, are rewarded with healthy children who grow up to become healthy adults.

THREE PATHS TO RESPONSIBLE PARENTING

If you have been making some of the same "good" parenting mistakes I have made, along with thousands of other mothers and fathers nationwide, don't despair. This book is focused on three main ideas that will help you recognize and manage your symptoms of co-dependency. The tools needed for recovery are available to everyone: perseverance, strength, and the courage to work hard to change your behavior and thus your child's future. These three main ideas are:

1. Parents need to understand and accept that they are the most important role models their children will ever have.

2. Parents need to know and accept that most parents are co-dependent to some degre; with that knowledge, they can begin the process of identifying their symptoms.

3. Parents need to understand that recovery from co-dependency is possible and to understand what recovery really means.

Being a parent is a complex task and is connected to many factors. Likewise, the three main issues of this book are interconnected and will overlap at times. For example, my own symptoms of co-dependency cut across several chapters: I have been a workaholic parent who didn't have time for my son, a hypercritical parent, and an overprotective parent who has paid my adult son's debts and misrepresented his less-than-honorable intentions to a number of would-be girlfriends. As I cannot be neatly categorized, neither can you. Although *The Co-Dependent Parent* will present five different models of dysfunctional family life in chapters 3 through 7, you will likely recognize bits and pieces of your co-dependent patterns of behavior in each of those chapters.

Parents as Role Models

As a mother or father, you will continue to have an impact on the emotional life of your daughter or son long after your death. As a parent, you are the most important role model your child will ever have. The family is a complex system in which every member's development is in some significant ways related to every other member's development—especially in the interaction between parent and child. Family therapist Virginia Satir, formerly with the Mental Research Institute in Palo Alto, California, explains in her chapter "Family Systems and Approaches to Family Therapy" in the anthology, *Family Therapy: An Introduction to Theory and Technique*:

> You arrived where you are right now and became the person you are at this moment in time because of a three-person learning system—a male and a female forebear, and yourself. If you did not actually have one of these persons on the premises, their images were on the premises. We also know that every child comes into this world only with the ingredients to grow and not a blueprint already developed.

Satir goes on to say that this blueprint has to be worked out for the child by the parents as they go along: "obviously, the blueprint depends upon the way in which the male and the female adult [the parents] hand down, or over, to their child the directions for how he is to grow." So, as parents we are the primary architects of our child's blueprint for growth. To that end, the blueprint that we develop for our child becomes a foundation that will last a lifetime. That blueprint, however, is based upon the blueprint we assimilated from our parents and, for that reason, may or may not serve our children well. In every chapter of *The Co-Dependent Parent* you will be reminded of how your behavior shapes the behavior of your child, and how you will be emulated or rejected by your son or daughter even when you are not aware of the messages you send.

Are You a Co-Dependent Parent?

Often we are not the role models for our children that we would like to be. Sometimes we understand where we went wrong and sometimes we don't. Sometimes we even think we're doing the right thing for our children but find out later that we triggered a reaction in our offspring that was the precise reaction we were trying to avoid. Chapters 3 through 7 describe in detail five models of dysfunctional families whose members are clearly co-dependent in a variety of ways: (1) the Demanding Parent, (2) the Critical Parent, (3) the Overprotective Parent, (4) the Disengaging Parent, and (5) the Ineffective Parent.

Demanding, dictatorial parents give the message, "I am the boss and you are my subordinate." In this case, the child believes the parent is saying, "It doesn't matter what you think; do it my way."

Critical parents are demanding parents, but more than that, they give their children the message, "You don't do anything right"—and their children believe it.

Overprotective parents often try to compensate for all the things they didn't have during their childhood. Smothering, overprotective parents give their children the message, "You can't do it, at least not by yourself." These parents also frequently make the statement, "I don't want my child to do that. I wasn't permitted to do it."

Disengaging parents are unavailable or preoccupied. They may be too sick, too tired, or too busy. Disengaging parents are usually people who received very little, if any, parenting and attention as children. Because they were not adequately loved, loving is hard for them. They give their children the message, "You are not terribly important to me."

Ineffective parents are frequently alcoholic or drug-addicted; sometimes they physically or sexually abuse their child. These parents tend to ask their children to assume adult roles that are beyond their emotional range, such as raising younger brothers and sisters, getting Dad to bed after he has passed out, and calling work to lie for the parent. Ineffective parents abandon their children each time they use alcohol or drugs. The message these parents give is, "I am not able to give you what you need. I am overwhelmed."

Read this section of the book with a receptive mind, and don't be surprised if you recognize yourself in one or more of these chapters. Most of us are co-dependent parents on some level. Don't berate yourself for uncovering your status (self-flagellation is a co-dependent trait, by the way). Instead, you should congratulate yourself for the unveiling, since having the ability and courage to identify your symptoms of co-dependency is the first phase of the recovery process.

Understanding Recovery

Luckily, learning how to manage your co-dependent behavior is not magical, because if recovery involved some esoteric process, it would be less attainable. The good news, then, is that recovery is possible if you are willing to rely on a more down-to-earth resource that dwells within each of us—and that is courage. By turning every page of this book, you are challenging yourself to acknowledge the truth about your co-dependent symptoms and accept that they have had, to some degree, a negative impact on your child. All is not lost, however. Steven W. Cawdrey, headmaster and co-founder of Spring Creek Community, a Montana therapeutic boarding school, reports, "It has been my experience that virtually 100 percent of the time, when the parent changes, the child changes—no matter how old that child happens to be. I have seen adult children change dramatically for the better once the parents started to monitor their own co-dependent behavior."

To that end, as a parent, you will need to accept that you are human and that recovery does not mean you have reached a state of perfection. Quite the contrary. Healthy families need not be perfect, only courageous and knowledgeable enough to take on the challenge of managing their imperfections.

✓ CHAPTER 2

THE MANY FACES OF CO-DEPENDENCY

Co-dependency can take many forms. In *Parents Who Help Their Children Overcome Drugs*, I wrote about co-dependency from the point of view of parents who are coping with chemical-abusing children. Such parents are labeled co-dependent because they are "enablers"—mothers and fathers addicted to the addictive behavior of their children. These are parents who need to be needed, so they enable their sons and daughters to use drugs by regularly coming to their rescue. Co-dependent parents make excuses to school authorities for homework undone and classes unattended by their drug-abusing children. They pay legal fees and court costs to prevent their offspring from having to face the negative consequences of drug addiction and drug-related crime. This type of co-dependent "help" allows the child to continue to use drugs.

Substance abuse by a child, however, is only one symptom that triggers co-dependent behavior between parent and child. There are, in fact, many faces of parental co-dependency, though every example involves at least one parent's pattern of dependence on the existence of a child who acts out feelings of low self-worth. In other words, a co-dependent parent literally requires interaction with a child whose behavioral patterns are either covertly or overtly self-denigrating. Such children have poor feelings about themselves because they are insecure. Ironically, co-dependent parents are themselves insecure people who are trying to cope with diminished self-esteem. So, to momentarily feel better about themselves, they practice co-dependency by implicitly or explicitly controlling the lives of their offspring for the purpose of making their son "better off," or "building their daughter's character." Either way, such parents are sustained temporarily by the belief that they must be valuable individuals since they are needed so badly by their offspring.

Co-dependency between parents and children is a tricky relationship to identify because of what is fundamentally involved in raising a child. Babies, for example, are by definition dependent on their parents to take care of them, so the parent-child relationship begins with the parent in a position of control. Symptoms of co-dependency emerge if the parent does not gradually relinquish that role as the child grows up. But diagnosing the problem can be difficult because of the subtle symptoms displayed by both parent and child.

Sometimes co-dependent behavior is centered around a parent's compulsion to be overly critical of his child, and the child's compulsion to live up to the parent's expectations. In this instance, the critical parent is self-cast as a hero because he assumes that his child needs the criticism in order to get (and stay) on the right track. With time, many of these children come to believe that their parents are correct, and generally try that much harder to please, which proves to be a never-ending struggle. Such sons and daughters tend to see themselves as lifelong failures no matter what they have achieved.

Another example of co-dependency is the parent "taking care of the child" by making virtually all of the offspring's decisions, so that the child becomes too fearful to control his own life and thus learns to rely on parental interference. As the child grows older, he becomes more and more needy; often, he demands that the parent manage his life. The child is ill-equipped to do otherwise since he has developed few life skills. Thus, co-dependent parents who raise dependent offspring typically find themselves continuing the pattern of support into the child's adult years. Although such parents may complain, in truth what they end up with is what they have worked hard to achieve: incompetent children who will request their support and allow their affairs to be controlled by their parents for the rest of their lives.

My co-dependent behavior toward my son was caused by guilt because I was absent so much during his childhood. I had set career goals for myself that didn't really leave time to nurture and parent my child until he was a teenager. I travelled a lot and often worked 13-hour days to stay in the "fast lane" where I could earn a high salary and lofty professional recognition. I rationalized that the hard work would pay off for my son because it would empower me to provide the "best" for him in terms of our economic status. I also convinced myself that my workaholism would prove to be a great role model because he would revere hard work and never be lazy. In sum, I believed (or wanted to believe) that my ambition was all for him.

As my son grew older, memories of my lack of parental nurturing began to plague me. My way of handling that guilt was to spend too much money on inappropriate gifts for my son. I also spent large sums bailing him out of financial trouble—primarily paying the fines and warrants for parking and traffic tickets that he neglected to pay. Thus, I established a co-dependent pattern of behavior that raised my son's level of material expectations to unrealistic proportions. He also came to expect that I would always be there to bail him out of difficult situations. One consequence is that his finances are very shaky because of his credit card debts and other excessive expenditures racked up over the years—all of which allowed him to live a lifestyle he could ill afford.

Although no drug problems were involved in our co-dependent relationship, my son and I still met the classic framework for the dysfunction of co-dependency: We were addictive personalities depending on each other's neediness. I needed to shower my son with impractical gifts and pay his parking fines because of my guilt over not nurturing him during his early years. My co-dependent behavior became an absolution of sorts, my unhealthy way of starting over, of making up for past mistakes.

My intentions, then, were admirable. On another level, though, my methods were self-serving, especially since my emphasis was placed on buying my way out of an uncomfortable situation rather than taking on the hard task of learning how to really nurture my son. My son became an addictive personality in response to my behavior. His need to maintain an image that required him to live beyond his means was tied to what he learned from my co-dependent method of substituting material goods for genuine nurturing.

Co-dependency, then, has many faces. What this book demonstrates is that the diverse range of co-dependent behavioral patterns that exist between parent and child can, in fact, be changed to reflect a healthy dynamic. I am working on my own recovery program to manage my co-dependency. Overcoming denial has been the biggest obstacle for me, because I found it hard to admit to my imperfections. Indeed, for many of the parents I interviewed, facing the fact that they had made some mistakes in the way they had raised their children was not easy. Yet, as one parent reported, "It might sound crazy, but now I'm glad that my husband and I had the courage to face up to our co-dependency. We're much better parents for it, and our children have certainly benefited from our efforts to change."

Recovery isn't as elusive as you may think. Recovery is directly related to your ability to call forth the confidence and strength to identify your co-dependent patterns of behavior and then learn to manage the way you behave. This book will help you accomplish both goals and thus establish a healthy relationship with your offspring. Don't despair if you recognize yourself in the examples of co-dependency already cited or yet to come. That's an excellent sign that your recovery process has gotten off to a good start. To help you gain an awareness of how you might be hurting yourself and your child, the next section will examine the unhealthy behaviors that are common to virtually all co-dependent families.

DYSFUNCTIONAL FAMILIES AND THE THREE "DON'Ts"

Years ago, when a series of crises hit all at once—my father died, my second marriage ended, I experienced on-the-job burnout—I hit bottom and started my recovery process. At that time, the term "co-dependent" was not used to describe my symptoms. My behavior, though, was that of a classic co-dependent parent who dominated a very dysfunctional family.

Sometimes it is not difficult to recognize that you are in a dysfunctional family if the symptoms are obvious and universally accepted; the mother or father is a substance abuser, for example, or one parent physically abuses a child or spouse. For most of us parents, though, our symptoms of dysfunction are very subtle, and we run co-dependent households without knowing what we are really teaching our children and how we may be harming them. For example, some years ago I appeared to be the consummate professional woman who was managing a successful career, raising a teenage son, and handling a dissolving marriage with enviable aplomb. I dressed impeccably. I was ambitious and aggressive. I maintained rigid standards that underpinned my behavior and that of my son. Those standards, however, included the three basic unspoken teachings of dysfunctional families: don't talk, don't feel, don't trust. Don't talk about what is really going on at home or within yourself; don't express what you really feel; and, above all, don't trust anybody, because everyone else is operating as dishonestly as you are.

I taught my son these co-dependent axioms, which I acted out every day. I hated my life and was miserable, but to say anything to anyone about what I was really feeling went against the "don't talk" tenet in which I believed. I also was careful not to show what I was feeling. Every morning, in a dark house with all window coverings closed to shut out the light, I prepared to go to work. My shoulders were slumped until I stepped outside my front door, at which point I took a deep breath, stood erect, placed a smile on my face, and provided the world with the image that everything was okay. I was charming and everyone at work liked me.

When I returned home at the end of the day, however, I immediately went to bed and literally pulled the covers over my head.

What I have since learned is that my behavior during that period fit the profile of the typical co-dependent: I had an inflated sense of self; I distrusted most everyone; I had a tendency to lie; I was very judgmental; and I separated myself from others as much as possible. I believed in my own grandiosity since I knew how unhappy I was; my ability to deceive others proved how superhuman I must be. On the other hand, I didn't trust anyone because I was so uncomfortable with my dishonesty that I feared every person I came in contact with would be the one to uncover my ruse of well-being. During this period, I was extremely critical of others to deflect attention from my own failures. Apart from business encounters with professional associates, I avoided contact with people and thus spent virtually all of my free time at home, alone.

I was a parent who was afraid most of the time. I first criticized my son continually, unfairly, and then sent him to live with his father during this period, because I simply could not cope with my life. I felt a lot of pain based on low self-esteem. To be open and honest would have meant revealing the "real me," and I assumed if that happened people would not like what they saw. It has taken me a long time to overcome that belief and discover my real self, because of my own upbringing and the roles I was "assigned" as a child and young adult.

HAMMERING SQUARE PEGS INTO ROUND HOLES HURTS

In co-dependent households, the children frequently act out the dysfunction of the family, especially when co-dependent parents unconsciously or consciously assign them roles that predetermine their behavior patterns. Children are expected to play these roles whether or not the roles fit their talents, abilities, or temperament.

Virtually every parent has an image in mind of the ideal child. Family therapist Virginia Satir argues that we got these ideas from what we were not, from what our parents did not do properly, and from how our parents told us we ought to be. "Everybody wants things to fit their ideals, so each adult applies these same things to his child when he comes along, and we think this is one of the ways that social heredity takes place," Satir states in "Family Systems and Approaches to Family Therapy," an essay in the book *Family Therapy: An Introduction to Theory and Technique*. The role playing that takes place in dysfunctional families generally reflects a co-dependent parent's fantasy. Reality, however, rarely supports a fantasy for long. In fact, Satir asserts that symptoms tend to break out when the "reality can no longer sustain the fantasy."

If, for example, a parent is pushing one child to play the role of hero, the results could be unpleasant as the fantasy collides with reality. The child herself could rebel and refuse to be the ideal child. The child could capitulate now, but later cast off the burden of the hero role as she reaches adulthood and begins to chafe under the pressure of having to be the great achiever. As long as this child strives to be the hero of the family, her sibling, relieved of having to carry that load, will fight for attention another way: the sibling will become the scapegoat who rebels against the parents' every desire.

Role playing of this sort takes place because all families are systems in which the behavior of one member is related to the behavior of all others. In essence, I took my cues on how to behave from my mother, father, sister, and brother. My siblings did likewise, and their development depended as well on how I related to each of them. If a co-dependent parent holds sway over the family, that parent's dysfunctional behavior will be felt by all and, in turn, will influence everyone's behavior. On the other hand, when a co-dependent parent begins a recovery program and stops hammering square pegs into round holes by implicitly or explicitly pressuring the child to play inappropriate roles, all members of the family can be expected to change for the better as they gain the freedom to discover their real selves.

To that end, there is an upside to this role playing: the more the child acts out, the better the opportunity the family has to heal its dysfunctions. Steven W. Cawdrey, who has worked with dysfunctional families for 10 years at his therapeutic boarding school in Montana, explains: "No matter how your son or daughter is acting out, that child is actually helping the family by bringing the family's dysfunction into the light."

As discussed earlier, every dysfunctional family is hiding from some type of emotional pain, which is why such families assiduously practice the three "don'ts"—don't talk, don't feel, don't trust. In my family, my father's compulsive gambling was rarely discussed, so there was no opportunity for us children to release the pain we felt concerning the hardships and embarrassments we experienced because of his addiction. That pain, along with the pain I felt because I had to suppress my reactions to other family secrets, is what fueled my angry acting out as an adolescent. My acting out, in turn, was inextricably tied to the role I was assigned by my parents during childhood, an emotionally uncomfortable role that added to my general malaise: I was the scapegoat, the rebel. What my father did not have the nerve to say or do to my mother, he coached me to say or do. Not too long after I moved out, my younger sister took over that role and began to rebel against my mother. My sister also was encouraged on the sidelines by my father.

Once I left home, however, I no longer needed to overtly fight my mother, so I became a superachiever. On the face of it, this made me look like a hero, but in retrospect, my superwoman behavior was another more subtle form of rebellion—it was my way of turning up my nose at my mother, of displaying one-upmanship on a grand scale. Many years later, when I was able to honestly analyze my role playing, I discovered that my acting out had always been rooted in some type of emotional pain. My experience was not unique. In fact, the existence of pain is a factor in each of the four primary examples of roles that children from co-dependent households tend to play: the hero, the scapegoat, the lost child, and the mascot.

The Hero

Though I felt inadequate most of the time, the role I played as a young adult was that of the hero. I was a workaholic, an overachiever who became a disengaging parent, which is typical of most adults assigned the hero's role.

By outer appearance, the heroes of most dysfunctional families look as if they have it all together. The hero child is typically a perfectionist, success-oriented, driven, and responsible. This is the child who works the hardest to keep the family together or to keep peace in the family.

When my mother divorced my father, for example, I left my graduate studies to move in with my father to help him cope with the breakup and to be responsible for stabilizing the family (my sister and brother, still minors, opted to live with Father).

Looking back, I realize that was not my responsibility. But part of the role I played had been to act out my father's dysfunction, which involved his abdication of parental authority. My father was quick to maneuver adult responsibilities onto the oldest child residing at home. At times my sister caught the brunt of his ineffectiveness, and at times when I was the eldest child in residence I found myself making decisions about the family that were emotionally above my head.

I also acted out the hero's role when I worked to attain my bachelor's degree. At that time I was driven by a desire for exceptional academic performance. I made myself carry seven and eight classes a semester to graduate with honors in 2½ years. Still, I felt inadequate, as do most heroes. And, like the typical hero, I also felt isolated, lonely, and afraid. But I continued at such a pace because I felt I could win my parents' approval and love if I was a "bionic" woman, and because I felt in competition with an older half-brother, a son my father had sired prior to his marriage to Mother.

Some years earlier I had witnessed a number of debates between my mother and father over who was the smartest and most likely to do well in college—my half-brother or myself. Mother supported my innate abilities over her stepson's accomplishments. My father touted how well his oldest son was already doing in college and questioned whether I would ever enroll, given the fact that before my 18th birthday I had married, had a child, and left my husband. In retrospect, I see that those parental debates proved to be a turning point for me, since shortly after my parents' exchange, my assigned role changed from that of scapegoat to hero.

The Scapegoat

Children who serve as the family scapegoat typically are defiant and angry. They are the rebels of the family and are the most likely to have an early pregnancy, become drug abusers, or threaten suicide. Generally, the scapegoat is acting out anger that is being suppressed by one or the other parent. My father, for example, did not like my mother's domineering personality at times. So he taught *me* how to rebel against her. I became the warrior he would not be. Ironically, like most scapegoats, I was angry with my father as well as my mother, although on the face of it my father and I were best buddies. Deep down I resented the fact that I was doing his dirty work, and there were many occasions when I felt guilty about the tactics I employed to cause my mother pain.

Scapegoats generally become argumentative adults who start fights with everyone about anything. A scapegoat may have problems keeping a job or a relationship because she has not learned how to deal in a healthy fashion with authority figures. In addition, an adolescent-scapegoat-turned-adult who is not in recovery is still seeking to please her parent by continuing to fight the fights that her parent shied away from. Despite their rebelliousness, scapegoat children are quite fearful and feel lonely and isolated, as do their heroic siblings.

Most of my adolescence was spent in rebellion. I was very angry with my mother's tight control of my life. I also was very angry with my father because he wouldn't stand up to Mother and used me, instead, to confront her. When I was about to be spanked, for instance, Father instructed me on the best way to "get back at" Mother. He suggested that I hold back my tears no matter how bad I hurt, because "it will hurt your mother more if she can't see that she's hurt you."

As I grew older, I was subtly encouraged to play the rebel or the scapegoat role as the hero's spot was assigned to my younger sister. She came along 10½ years after I was born, and I resented her presence. I believed she was prettier than I, and I was jealous of the attention she got. So I acted out the scapegoat role as she played the hero, which allowed us both to get a lot of attention. Interestingly, when I became a young adult and opted to become the hero, my sister started using drugs within a few years of my role reversal and became the family scapegoat. My brother, on the other hand, has been the lost child, as best as I can tell, throughout his life.

The Lost Child

From the outside, the lost child exhibits a false maturity. This child is quiet, a loner, the type that most would consider shy. Often, the lost child gets sick or injured to get noticed, which is just what the co-dependent parent wants, because there is something going on in the family that this parent doesn't want to face. Tending to a sick child becomes a legitimate excuse for this parent to avoid the more unpleasant issue. In addition, the parent uses guilt to exercise a great deal of control over the lost child by routinely reminding the child how much has been sacrificed for his well-being. To that end, these children are typically spoiled and overprotected by the parent who is in hiding. The lost child also feels inadequate, lonely, and fearful, and carries around a great deal of pain and guilt. Because he has been so pampered, the lost child is apt to lack many life skills as an adult.

My younger brother fits this category. He is the quiet, low-key member of the family, though he has generated quite a bit of excitement and attention over the years because of his many ailments and accidents. He suffered from a serious case of asthma, had a skin disorder that caused his feet to peel raw at times, broke his nose from using the bed as a trampoline, poisoned himself by eating insect repellent, and gave himself a concussion when he hit his head in a schoolyard fall.

The Mascot

A friend of mine who has two children treats the younger one as the family hero and complains constantly about the antics of the other. The elder son is hyperactive and the class clown, yet he is emotionally fragile and experiences bouts of depression. He often brings home strange friends and will do almost anything to get attention. He exhibits classic symptoms attributed to the role of the mascot. The mascot wants to embarrass his parents, though that is rarely admitted. Such children are angry with one or both parents.

Scapegoat children overtly act out anger; mascots act out a covert form of rebellion. They, too, are subtly encouraged by one or the other parent to "perform" what are really hostile acts that are disguised to appear as harmless pranks or incidents. The mascot's comedic actions almost always get the child into trouble, however, and throw the family into an uproar. Children who play the role of mascot feel a lot of fear, pain, and guilt. Like scapegoat children, mascots feel anger toward the parent with whom they are in unspoken collusion. They feel used by this parent, although outward appearances would indicate otherwise. They also feel enormous guilt for their actions toward the parent who is under covert attack.

Many mascots grow up to become all-consuming people-pleasers who resent the people they go out of their way to please.

THE CO-DEPENDENT PARENT CREDO: "MY CHILD NEEDS FIXING"

Parenthood is the most important on-the-job training experience a person could ever have. The majority of us don't bring a body of expertise to the child-rearing task—especially the first time out. We learn instead by trial and error. Nonetheless, many of us believe that effective parenting requires us to be perfect, or at least to maintain the image of perfection. It does not. But there is so much heroic mythology associated with parenthood, it's hard not to attempt to fit an idyllic role. There is also much guilt associated with the mandate to do the best for your child. As parents, all eyes are on us. We hear from in-laws, teachers, doctors, and friends if our children misbehave. So we tend to demand the "ideal" from ourselves as parents, and we expect our sons and daughters to represent us well. When our children don't, it's hard for most of us co-dependent parents to accept the fact that we contributed in some way to what went wrong.

To that end, a valuable lesson was reaffirmed for me not long ago during a conversation I struck up with a medical doctor seated next to me on a plane. I had been out of town giving a speech about how parents can help their children overcome drugs. The doctor, it turns out, had been a member of my audience. During the course of the conversation I discovered that he was divorced and had custody of a 16-year-old daughter who was recovering from a substance-abuse problem. His daughter's recovery didn't begin until he realized that he needed to change his co-dependent approach to child-rearing as much as his child needed to give up drugs. "At first, when I attended counseling sessions with my daughter I believed that my child needed fixing, not me," he recounted with a grin. These days, this proud parent reports, he is an active participant in family counseling and has changed dramatically—he doesn't try to control his daughter's life, as was his practice in the past.

What this father eventually understood was how a dysfunctional family headed by a co-dependent parent operates: A child who is acting out unhealthy, disruptive behavior is not behaving that way in a vacuum, because the very presence of co-dependency dictates that there are at least two players participating in a destructive dynamic. In other words, if your child is displaying dysfunctional patterns of behavior, as a parent you have some relationship to and responsibility for the child's acting out.

MIRROR, MIRROR ON THE WALL...

None of us is perfect. All of us have made some mistakes in the way we raised our children; our mothers and fathers made some mistakes in the way they raised us. Effective parenting doesn't require perfection. Instead, it requires our willingness to acknowledge where there are weaknesses so that we can learn how to manage our imperfections. This concept is simple enough, but very difficult to implement. Most co-dependent parents were raised by co-dependent parents, and thus lack role models for what constitutes a healthly family environment. It's hard, then, for most of us to recognize our own symptoms of co-dependency. The following list, prepared by teachers of the La Puente–Hacienda (California) School District who provide effective parenting instruction to men and women in Los Angeles County jails, describes common characteristics of adults who were raised by co-dependent parents.

- They judge themselves mercilessly.
- They have difficulty having fun.
- They take themselves very seriously.
- They have difficulty with intimate relationships.
- They overreact to changes over which they have no control.
- They constantly seek approval and affirmation.
- They lie when it would be just as easy to tell the truth.
- They are extremely loyal even in the face of evidence that the loyalty is undeserved.
- They are either super-responsible or super-irresponsible.

- They have difficulty following a project through from beginning to end.
- They guess at normal behavior, since they have had no role models to demonstrate what healthy interaction is.
- They are impulsive and tend to lock themselves into a course of action without giving serious consideration to alternative behaviors or possible consequences.
- They usually feel that they are different from other people.

Did you recognize yourself? I did when I first read these symptoms of co-dependency, and my initial reaction was to want to run away. The list represented a mirror that reflected a painful image of myself. I felt anger toward my own parents for having contributed to my co-dependency. I also wondered whether it was possible to change my co-dependent behavior and, if so, whether the effort would be worthwhile. I was shaken when it occurred to me that my son could one day read this list and become angry with me, since these symptoms of co-dependency could just as easily apply to him as an adult if I didn't gather the strength to break the cycle. Are you feeling some of the same feelings? Are you thinking some of the same thoughts? Good. That means you have already started your recovery process. But be patient. Recovery is a gradual process.

Your questions and concerns will be addressed as you move through each chapter in this book, but I will answer one bottom-line question now. Through talking to family members nationwide and by garnering the strength to begin my own recovery process, I have learned this: recovery *is* worth the effort. As individual parents we deserve healthy lives, and our children deserve the best we have to offer. This book will help you begin your journey.

PART 2

COMMON LEGACIES OF PAIN

Part Two presents five co-dependent parenting models in Chapters 3 through 7: (1) the demanding parent, (2) the critical parent, (3) the overprotective parent, (4) the disengaging parent, and (5) the ineffective parent. Few of us fit perfectly into any one of these models. Still, categorizing co-dependent parenting in this way is useful because it helps us see ourselves as our children see us and thus begin to recognize how our every action impacts the character development of our offspring.

As you read the descriptions of co-dependent parenting, you may be dismayed to realize that they mirror your own situation. You may be tempted to deny what you know is true, to pretend that none of the models match your behavior. Maintain your openness, though, and do the exercises found at the end of each chapter in Part Two. Your family's well-being could depend upon your courage and willingness to acknowledge your co-dependency and to begin your recovery by completing these exercises. The usefulness and ultimate purpose of the exercises will be clarified in Part Three: Recovery—Taking Action, Breaking Patterns.

CHAPTER 3

THE DEMANDING PARENT

I was a demanding parent with a rigorous vision of what I wanted my son's future to look like. I knew how I wanted him to dress and express himself, what I wanted him to read, and what type of girl I wanted him to date. My notions about his future were steeped in the best of intentions: that my only child should become a prosperous young man and marry an equally successful young woman. Often I imagined that my son, a talented basketball player, would play ball professionally and that I would be interviewed on television as the behind-the-scenes power that had led to his career achievements. I was determined that when that moment came, my son would prove to be an intelligent spokesperson and role model for young people interested in becoming sports professionals—and I would be viewed by parents nationwide as the ideal mother.

These days, because I understand more about my co-dependent patterns of behavior, I have learned to look more carefully at what I once believed were selfless motives. Of course I wanted good things to happen to my son; but I realize now that my demanding approach to child-raising had as much to do with what I thought I might gain from his successes. Basically, I saw my son as an extension of myself. Thus, I wanted him to upgrade my image of myself by accomplishing more than I had achieved and by placing me in the limelight so that I could finally get the attention I craved because of my own dysfunctional upbringing. Ironically, what I did to my son—by maintaining a demanding, dictatorial demeanor—was what my mother had done to me, and the results, unfortunately, were much the same. I had left home when I was 15 to marry and have a child. My son finished high school at 17, moved out on his own, impregnated two girls within a few years, and has attended college only sporadically.

My behavior, then, was similar to my mother's. And both my mother and I behaved like thousands of other parents who try to insist that their sons and daughters live their lives in ways that are "acceptable" to the parents. Such parents do not anticipate that their co-dependent approach to child rearing can adversely impact their children's self-esteem.

My sister summed up our upbringing recently in this way: "In our household, what we felt meant absolutely nothing." For my sister, this attitude translated into low self-esteem that still persists at age 28. A feeling of inadequacy has been difficult for me to overcome as well. Although I am 39 years old, I still find myself seeking my mother's approval all too often. Why? For children of demanding parents, the logic that underpins our feelings goes like this: If our mother does not think much of our opinions or actions, then our opinions or actions cannot be worth much. And if our opinions or actions are not worth much, how can our mother love us? Finally, if our mother does not love us, how can we be worth anything?

"I AM THE BOSS AND YOU ARE MY SUBORDINATE"

In the classic demanding parent model, dictatorial, demanding parents give the message, "I am the boss and you are my subordinate." The child interprets this to mean, "Your thoughts don't count, things are going to be done my way." Such demanding parents do not teach their children to make choices; they make most of their children's decisions for them. Because they are not allowed to make their own mistakes, the offspring of these parents fail to learn essential life skills and lessons. Living with a demanding parent is like being sentenced to life in prison. The parent, like a prison guard, always has the last word. In a prison environment, it would be difficult to convince the inmates that the guards love them. It's also a pretty tough sell to convince the children of demanding parents that their mothers and fathers love them. In addition, these children have a hard time genuinely liking their parents.

Demanding parents push their children to achieve goals that are sometimes impossible or, at the very least, will require great sacrifices in time and effort. In other words, demanding parents want to assign their children the hero's role, whether or not their sons and daughters are up to the task or have any desire to play that part. Such parents push because they fear that their offspring will not "turn out" as planned, and that would reflect on the parents' abilities and reputation. One result of this controlling, co-dependent behavior is that demanding parents tend to raise children who either become doormats or rebels. A child from this kind of family may retreat into shyness and take on the role of the lost child, who is really very lonely while displaying a false mask of maturity (as my brother did). Or, such a young person may become the family scapegoat, defiant and acting out anger—often through early pregnancy (as I did), chemical addiction (as my sister did), or through suicide threats and attempts (as did both my sister and myself).

In general, the three of us children acquiesced to some of my mother's demands and rebelled against others. By graduating from college I fulfilled one of my mother's "conditions." But I got pregnant when I was only 16, was divorced twice by the time I was 30, and was financially bankrupt by my 35th birthday. My sister adhered to my mother's vision of how her life should unfold by enrolling in college. However, she eventually dropped out and did not obtain a degree, has been a drug addict for a number of years, and is the unemployed and unmarried mother of a two-year-old son. My brother, 24, finished high school, served a number of years in the armed forces, and recently secured an upwardly mobile, professional position at a large corporation. His personal history, however, is another matter. He is already divorced, and my mother has caught him physically attacking one of his girlfriends.

Another dysfunctional behavior exhibited by the children of demanding parents is lying. They may look directly into the eyes of their mother or father, nod in agreement, and then do exactly the opposite of what they have agreed to do. Often these children become skilled liars, since they begin to practice deception at such a young age. Some become so good at not telling the truth that they begin to believe their own lies and no longer deal with reality.

Demanding parents, then, go too far when they set rigid standards for their children. By so doing, they contribute to a harmful, co-dependent familial dynamic that generally produces the opposite of what they desire for their offspring. My mother certainly did not want us children to make the mistakes that we have made. As a mother myself, I did not want to become a grandmother twice before my son completed college and before I turned 40. Yet, I was in large part the architect of my son's future, as my mother was of mine.

BECOMING AWARE

Both my mother and I have learned our lessons. Nowadays, my mother no longer demands us children do anything. I no longer push my son so that I can daydream about attaining future celebrity status through his career achievements. And we pay close attention to co-dependent language in the phrases we routinely express. Are you a demanding parent? Is your spouse a demanding parent? If you are still not sure, read the following list of statements demanding parents make to their children. I squirmed a bit when I first read this list, which was developed by the teachers from the Hacienda–La Puente School District for their parenting program taught in Los Angeles County jails.

- "Not right now."
- "Do it now!"
- "Clean up your room now!"
- "Because I said so."
- "That's my rule. That's why."
- "No, because I said so. You don't need a reason."
- "Get over here and do what I tell you."
- "Stop it!"
- "I said to do it, so do it!"

As this list indicates, demanding parents believe they are always right. Confident that their way of doing things is by definition the best way, they behave like tyrants. Such parents cultivate an image of being all-knowing and indestructible. In truth, these mothers and fathers typically are very fearful people who seek to control their children and family life in order to feel safe. Often they themselves had dysfunctional childhoods during which they were subject to the unpredictable whims of rigid or emotionally volatile parents.

Brenda and Chuck, the parents of this chapter's family profile, follow such a pattern. Brenda was raised by a mother who had difficulty expressing her feelings, particularly anger. So she would explode—sometimes violently—from time to time, always when least expected. Chuck was raised by a classically demanding father who rode roughshod over both Chuck (an only child) and his mother. Both Brenda and Chuck admit that their upbringing influenced the way they raised their children. Chuck, however, is more forthright than Brenda in talking about the role he played in the family and in daughter Amber's dysfunctional behavior. He admits that he was a demanding parent, and he feels that Brenda was every bit as demanding as he was, if not more so. Brenda, on the other hand, confesses that she is still in the dark as to how her style of parenting could have produced such drastic results in Amber, who rebelled against her parents' demands by becoming a substance abuser and a self-mutilator at age 12.

Brenda's view of herself seems considerably more benign than the way she is regarded by the rest of the family. She doesn't see herself as being a particularly demanding parent. As you read what she has to say, withhold your assessment of whether Brenda and Chuck were demanding parents until you have read the testimony of all four family members. This family is recovering at its own pace, and some members see themselves and their history more clearly than do others.

FAMILY PROFILE:

Brenda, Chuck, Amber, and Linda

Chuck, 48, is a university professor and neurophysiologist who makes his living observing the electrical activity of the epileptic brain. On the home front, however, it took drastic behavior on the part of his youngest daughter, Amber, now 15, to get him to observe the dysfunctional dynamics that prevailed in his household. "I would not have recognized my co-dependency had it not been for my daughter," Chuck reports. His 45-year-old wife, Brenda, a teacher of physically handicapped children, agrees: "I still don't understand what happened to Amber, but I do know that if it weren't for her acting out, we all would be going along just as we had for 20 years." Amber's "acting out" consisted of alcohol abuse at 12 and cocaine addiction by the time she was 13. She also carved self-deprecating comments on her arms and legs with razor blades and safety pins.

Amber's crisis was the impetus that got Brenda and Chuck into family counseling sessions where they began to recognize their patterns of co-dependent parenting, much of which was behavior they had learned from their parents. Brenda and Chuck have been married 22 years and live in an affluent suburb of Southern California. They have one other child, 17-year-old Linda. Amber describes her older sister as playing the role of hero in the family, in contrast to Amber's scapegoat or rebel persona.

Brenda

"I had a stable family who loved me and was always there for me," Brenda recalls, though she admits that she was raised in a co-dependent household. Brenda attributes much of the downside of her childhood to flaws in her mother's personality, rather than her father's. "My mother was a follower. She was warm but she was volatile. She was not comfortable in expressing her feelings. So she craved things that she could have had easily, but she was not at all demanding about these things. For much of her life she seemed to be very frustrated." Sometimes, Brenda remembers, her mother would get so frustrated that "she would get to a point where she couldn't hold back what she felt, then she would grab a broom and chase us kids through the house."

Brenda's mother was particularly frustrated with her marriage—even on her deathbed, 10 years ago. "She told me, as she was dying and with my father in the room, that she wanted to have more communication with Father." Brenda's father was a workaholic and an entrepreneur who owned many small businesses during his lifetime. He enlisted his wife to work for these businesses whether she wanted to or not. She did a lot of her husband's bookkeeping—a line of work she did not like—and she was a waitress on occasion when Brenda's father happened to own a restaurant.

Brenda believes her mother's frustration was fueled as well by her father's unemotional nature. Brenda describes her father as a quiet, withdrawn Oklahoman who rarely expressed his feelings. Generally he accepted whatever life had to offer—the good and particularly the bad. She explains his stoic behavior as being directly related to his upbringing. "My father had malaria when he was in the second grade. Shortly after he recovered, his father died and my father had to quit school to take care of his two sisters. When his mother remarried, my father wasn't liked by his stepfather. So when his mother discovered she was dying, she called her 12-year-old son—my father—aside to tell him that he had better get out of the home. With that warning, my father was on his own by the time he was 13 years old."

Similarly, Brenda understands her mother's need for emotional closeness as based on the circumstances of her upbringing. "The events that impacted my mother's family were traumatic and made them very close together, but also made them very, very co-dependent. They basically hovered over each other." Brenda's mother came from a family whose members were very protective of each other and "worshipped" their mother, because of the great misfortune the family had suffered along the way: The father was killed while his tenth child was still in his wife's womb; one of the children died of starvation not long after the family moved to the United States from Austria. The nine surviving offspring produced only five grandchildren, which Brenda attributes to their co-dependent lifestyle of clinging to each other. Five of the daughters, for example, never married and lived with their mother until her death at age 86.

In her assessment of her own upbringing, Brenda offers confusing testimony about her response to the virtues and weaknesses displayed by her parents. She tends to minimize her father's shortcomings and undervalue her mother's virtues. When questioned about the seeming imbalance in her point of view, Brenda does not deny that she has presented a distorted picture of her parents. Still, she reports almost wistfully that what she tells me is what she feels: "My father, who is 86 years old, is very kind and gentle and loving and caring," although she admits that he "never went out of his way to do special things. Instead, he just went to work, did his thing, and was always there." She adds, "I don't think Dad needed to show his feelings. I think he was so self-sufficient, so independent, he didn't need anyone else." Brenda admires many of her father's traits—so much so that she states outright, "I would prefer to be like him than like my mother, who was very volatile. I think I feel closer to my father than I ever did to my mother. I don't think I really liked all of my mother's character traits, although she was a nurturer and was warm and caring with us."

Brenda would have liked both of her parents to be "more open and outgoing. I think I would have been more open and warm and would have been able to show it more if they had been more outgoing, but Father didn't care anything about that kind of thing. Mother did, but only as it pertained to family. For my mother, if it wasn't family it didn't exist." Brenda also is regretful about her parents' unwillingness to display emotion. "When I was ready to go off to college, my mother later told me that she cried and cried and cried and that it was the hardest thing she had ever experienced, but I had no knowledge of that at all. So, again, instead of expressing her feelings openly, she didn't let me know. I would have learned to do more of that myself if they could have expressed themselves more openly."

Another legacy of her upbringing is that Brenda sees herself as someone who "doesn't want to say things that are painful. It's hard for me to say I was wrong, that I feel hurt or anything like that."

In Chuck, Brenda chose a husband who in emotional terms is similar to her parents, especially her father. Chuck does not readily show emotion, particularly anger. "Chuck is a person who can't handle anger, period. He'll squelch it; he just wants it gone at any cost. If you try to talk to him about it, he'll just change the subject, or put it into terms where it's intellectualized instead of emotional." Brenda admits that her two daughters have been harmed by Chuck's and her difficulty in handling emotions, but she is still confused as to how things could have gone so wrong for Amber.

"I still puzzle about what happened, about why we are where we are, although, logically, I've heard it explained many times. I saw all of us as just going along fine and then all of a sudden we started really having problems with Amber." Could the problems have been caused by some circumstance that sprang up overnight? "That's how it seems, but I know better than that; I know that it was long-term, starting with Chuck's and my problems. But I have a hard time seeing it. What I see with Amber is a child who has a very poor self-image, which came from somewhere— probably from her mother and father. Amber has a lot of oppositional behavior, and that probably comes from being in a family where expressing feelings, especially anger, is not okay—and I did always want my daughters to achieve a lot. Still," she adds with a tremor in her voice, "somehow I have a real hard time seeing that it could have been as bad as what I see manifested at home."

Brenda's and Chuck's agony over Amber's behavior began with a telephone call from a parent they did not know. This woman had been told of Amber's drug use by her son, a friend of Amber's who was concerned about what might happen to her. Until this call, Brenda says, she had no idea that Amber was using cocaine. "Chuck and I got on the line and talked to this parent, and when we hung up we went to the hospital that night to have Amber checked for cocaine. When the tests were completed, I will say one thing—Chuck gets credit for this—he said, 'We need help. This is not something I feel I can deal with.' "

Within two days Brenda and Chuck had researched the types of treatment programs available, pulled Amber from school, and placed her in a residential treatment facility in San Diego. Neither parent had any history of substance abuse in their family background. "I think that's why it made such an impression on us," Brenda says. The experience was a traumatic one for Brenda. "I can say honestly that the knot in my stomach, the pain I felt for Amber and with her, will never go away. The night that I had to leave Amber [in the residential treatment facility] was the worst night in my life. To go off and leave a 12-year-old with all of these strange people scared the hell out of me. I kept looking at her and thinking that I didn't know what this was all about."

What has she learned from the experience? "I feel that my parenting, my basic moral rules for myself are good and I have not changed them. I have realized that I need to let Amber and Linda experience and learn more without my being afraid of what they're going to do." Yet, the guidelines Brenda has established for her youngest daughter include these: "I want to know who Amber is with, I want to know where she is, and I want her to be home by 12 o'clock on Friday and Saturday nights. I'm very willing to drive her around to different places—then I know where she is and who she is with."

Brenda does have an Achilles heel. She is not as tough as some of her comments would indicate, which she readily acknowledges moments after giving a hard-nosed recital of how her household is run. "I feel confident about my parenting. I don't feel confident about being able to deal with Amber. She's a very, very strong personality. She can talk herself into or out of anything she wants, and I have a real, real hard time keeping up. And it bothers me, because I have a hard time following through. When I say something and I want it done, I have a hard time making sure it's done. That's a problem of mine. I don't feel I'm strong enough to deal with Amber."

Through attending family counseling sessions as part of Amber's drug treatment recovery program, Brenda has learned a lot about her own psyche and that of her husband and family. "Both Chuck and I have a lot of latent anger that is not expressed, even though we have spent the past year and one-half in counseling working on all of this—the anger is still there. I was totally unaware of all of this. Now I can see that there is a lot of anger in me that I don't express." These days, Brenda is trying to talk more, to be more open. "When I am talking to the girls and feel that I haven't completed a conversation or finished a thought or worked through a problem, I turn around and go to them to tell them how I'm feeling. I don't think I ever did that before and I'm still not doing it with Chuck yet, but I am doing it with the girls." Digging deeper, she admits that much of her life has been spent "other-directed" rather than "me-directed." "I work on the house instead of working on me." She says she is learning to give up that type of behavior, though, and can applaud her own progress: "I've come a long way from my mother."

Brenda's marriage has changed, also, though not entirely to her liking. "We are aware of our disagreements, whereas before they were so swallowed, they just didn't exist at all. I can see now that Chuck has a lot of anger in him too, and I would never, never have known that. I feel less comfortable with our relationship now than I did a couple of years ago, because we realize now that we do have anger and that we do have frustrations and that we do have disagreements, and before, none of this existed. I don't honestly know what the anger's about or where it comes from because I think that I have been basically happy. I would not change anything. I don't want to not live with Chuck. I don't want to not be in the family. I don't want to make any drastic changes. But I do think that the last year and the next few years to come are probably going to be the most difficult years of our lives together."

With respect to Amber's future, Brenda is cautiously optimistic. Now 15, Amber has changed a great deal from the 12-year-old who had to be placed in a residential drug treatment center. These days, "if Chuck and I really say, 'No, you cannot do that,' she'll say, 'Okay.' " Brenda adds, "Amber has not had any self-destructive behavior recently, though I still feel she has a poor self-image, but I don't think that's something that's going to change overnight." Some examples of Amber's low self-esteem reflect a rebellious attitude, a typical response of children of demanding parents. "She has her hair rainbow colors and she has to keep changing it, although her hair is brittle and damaged. I think this is a way of her trying to get approval from her peers. She's like a chameleon. If she's with one group of friends, she'll dress one way; if she's with another group of friends, she'll dress another way; and when she's with relatives, she dresses completely differently. I think it's her way of trying to be accepted. She also says she's too fat and she's not. She says she doesn't look good and she's beautiful. She says her feet are awful and they're fine. If I tell her, 'You look real nice,' she'll say, 'No, I don't.' "

In addition, Amber displays what Brenda refers to as "social cravings," meaning that Amber likes to be surrounded by all types of people— mainly boys. On the brighter side, from Brenda's point of view, Amber has started talking more positively about her future. "She says that she wants to do good things in life, though she does not follow through. She laughs a lot now, which I think is wonderful. She loves to sing, which I think is great. She seems to be happy. She's not cutting herself anymore, and she tends to show her anger and pain."

To that end, the family has instituted something they call the "Feelings Round," where they meet on Sunday afternoons to share what they are feeling. Each family member must speak a minimum of two minutes and no longer than five. No one is permitted to interrupt. Once the "round" has been completed and everyone has had an opportunity to speak, the family dicussion is open to any topic. Brenda believes this has been a worthwhile activity for the family, though it is hard sometimes to fit the Feelings Round into everyone's schedule. This way of sharing has been as helpful for Linda—the elder daughter who has played the hero's role in the family—as it has been for Amber. "Linda swallows everything—

all of her feelings," Brenda says. "But now she has a completely different understanding of the fact that other people are in pain, not just her, that other people have to deal with the same things she's dealing with. I think that she's gained a lot more insight; she shows a lot more maturity. At the time that Amber was acting out and was placed in a drug treatment facility, it showed up in Linda in that she just sat and stared at her schoolwork and folded on her final exams." Linda is doing well in school these days and has her mother's complete faith. "I'm happy with Linda. She drives my husband's car and I don't have to ask her where she's going. I trust her. We've never had any problems with her."

Linda was angry at her parents, however, when they insisted that she be transferred to another school when she did poorly on her finals during the crisis with Amber. With the wisdom of hindsight and the many evenings of group family counseling under her belt, Brenda admits that she and Chuck moved too soon. The difference in how they would handle such a circumstance today is probably a good measure of how much Chuck and Brenda have grown: "If Linda were in academic trouble these days we would say, 'Linda, what do *you* want to do?' "

Chuck

"Father heaped a lot of love on me. He was always assuring me that I was the apple of his eye," explains Chuck, an energetic and earnest-looking man who appears comfortable talking about his past, if not entirely sure that he understands it all. "But," he adds, "though you hear those things, actions speak louder than words." Chuck's father was a "sometimes raging individual," according to his only son. Chuck's perception of his upbringing is that both he and his mother—a quiet, passive person—were controlled by his father, an eighth-grade dropout who worked for the Southern Pacific Railroad. Chuck recalls how he was often screamed at and verbally abused by his father. There is one occasion he is particularly anxious to share: "I took some verbal abuse for doing some incompetent things as a kid. Once, for example, I was pretty little and had been given a dart game either for Christmas or for some other holiday. Somehow I managed to lose one of the darts. Father broke my dart gun in half for my punishment. I still remember how I felt that that was a pretty hard punishment for losing a dart. I felt it was so unfair." His mother's response to this and other confrontations with Chuck's father was to "just stand by." Chuck felt she was ineffectual.

Still, Chuck considers his upbringing to have been fundamentally good, though he states, "I think it was a co-dependent upbringing and, of course, my issues began from what I learned as a kid from my parents." Chuck learned primarily from his dad. "He issued the commandments around the house. Things had to be done a certain way—and only he knew how to do whatever needed to be done. Father felt that when I did things well, that reflected on him. So, I was always the good kid, the kid whose parents said, 'What a good boy.' But as I got older, I got angry." By the time Chuck reached high school age he "got tired of not being independent, of not doing things my own way." When he left a few years later for college, "I was ready and I was angry."

Chuck's relationship with his father softened as his father began to show the ravages of chronic leukemia. Chuck was 11 when his father's illness was diagnosed; he was 26 when his father died. As his father became more and more sick, Chuck says, he began to feel more and more guilt about his relationship with his dad. "Since I was in my twenties and no longer around my father, and because my father was sick, he was no longer the threat he had been. So I began to get close to him again in a way that I had not for years."

Chuck also believes he was able to warm up to his father during the last few years of his life because Chuck himself was becoming an independent person. "I was getting out on my own, doing things for myself, not being under my father's control. So I began to soften and feel better toward Father." Yet, Chuck admits that he hasn't entirely conquered the low self-esteem brought on by a childhood under the rigid rule of a demanding parent. To that end, he still has trouble showing his anger and admits that there are probably many co-dependent behaviors he has yet to uncover about himself. Nowadays, Chuck seems to be enjoying his and his family's recovery process and to be looking forward to sorting himself out. When he first sought help, his frame of mind was very different. "You don't go into therapy because you're a happy person. I was in agony because I was afraid my daughter was going to die."

Chuck also didn't understand the extent to which he was going to change in the months to come. He still has vivid recollections of his response to what he heard at the first few group parenting meetings he attended. "Parents were saying things like, 'My kid is doing fine. Her hair is orange now and she hangs out on Melrose, but she's not doing drugs,' and things like, 'My daughter does pretty well in school—she's getting C's.' I thought, when I heard such comments, 'Why do they let their children do that? Why? No way would I do that. I'm not that dumb. No way am I ever going to release my kid [from the drug treatment program] to do that kind of thing.'"

During that period, Chuck and Brenda sat in on their first Co-Anon meeting, a support group for family members who are coping with cocaine users. Again, he and Brenda were appalled by what they heard: "The Co-Anon meeting was full of people who lived with drug users, who were saying that they had learned to simply let it go—that the abuser was responsible for his or her actions. I thought, 'These people are crazy. They're just letting these addicts run over them. Why don't they do something?' "

At this point in the interview, Chuck laughs at his former point of view and adds, "It took months for Brenda and I to get with it." Chuck and his wife attended parent meetings four times a week. Still, "It took a long time with a lot of people sharing for us to understand how we had to change in order to help Amber and Linda." Chuck listened over and over to Melody Beattie's cassette tape based on her book, *Co-Dependent No More*, particularly the part about detachment. "Her message was that you have to detach and let go. So I started to try to detach, and by God, it felt good, it was so wonderful, because I started to think about myself and I stopped obsessing on Amber. It made me feel like an individual again, instead of someone who was being jerked around by a daughter who was out of control." Amber "always had to do something" to demand his attention, from "carving initials in her ankle to cutting her wrist with a razor blade."

Although Brenda is uncertain how Amber and the family reached such crisis levels, Chuck's point of view on these matters is quite clearcut: He believes that Amber's problems are a direct result of the way she was raised. In fact, he begins his description of what happened to Amber by describing both his and his wife's character traits. "I'm a passive-aggressive type; Brenda is a more aggressive-aggressive type. Brenda has great determination and has been a great help to me. She's been very encouraging. I might not have gone to graduate school to get my doctorate if not for her. But while she is very encouraging, she has been very outspoken about what she wanted me to do. So there is a lot of antagonism between us—both past and present. We fight a lot."

Moreover, though Chuck believes that "Brenda is even more controlling than I," he admits that they both are guilty of having been very controlling parents who pushed and pressured their daughters to meet unreasonable demands. "We didn't communicate a lot, we just kind of did what it came to us to do—our girls didn't breathe unless we were checking it out. We put a lot of pressure on them to be what we felt they should be, and we wanted both of our kids to be geniuses and get Ph.D.'s or M.D.'s.

No matter what, the kids had to make A's, even if we had to do the homework for them. Between the two of us we had a synergistic relationship that was focused on the kids, and the effect was to diminish their self-confidence."

Amber and Linda were sent to schools that catered to the mentally gifted. One such school required its students to have an IQ of 130 or more. Another of the girls' alma maters was a Baptist fundamentalist school that was rigid and highly structured, according to Chuck. This school was particularly good for Amber, he believes, because she has been diagnosed as having an attention deficit disorder (ADD). "Amber has a hard time remembering things and is unable to focus for long periods of time," Chuck explains. The two daughters were transferred from this school when Amber was entering the fifth grade. By the seventh grade, "things started getting bad with Amber, because there was no structure and because she was 12, almost a teenager, so she was beginning to become a different kid. Her grades started to drop and we started to exert a lot of pressure. Brenda and I had always exerted a lot of pressure, but then [when Amber's grades fell] we really exerted intense pressure, because Amber wasn't performing. She wasn't doing what she was supposed to do. She wasn't getting A's."

To Chuck, "exerting intense pressure" meant that "when you come home you do your homework. But the idea is, you don't sit down by yourself and do your homework, you come home and your mom and dad help you do your homework. Actually, when you come home they'll *do* your homework if you mess around until nine P.M. and it's still not done and there's a deadline. No matter what, your child is going to get an A, even if you have to do the work. I was a co-dependent."

Chuck was not alone in this co-dependent effort to make his children and thus himself look good. "My wife was *very* supportive," he says with a laugh. Their tactics didn't work with Amber, though; the problems kept getting worse. They started going to a therapist. When Amber was in the eighth grade, Chuck and Brenda, following the advice of the educational therapist, dug in even deeper. They established strict guidelines for how Amber was to behave, along with clear-cut punishments if she deviated from the prescribed behavior. Cooperation from Amber's teachers was also solicited—they had to provide weekly progress reports on her grades.

Amber's response to her parents' resolve was to become more and more angry and more antagonistic. The educational psychologist recommended that Chuck and Brenda engage the services of a psychiatrist. The psychiatrist suggested that Amber take Ritalin, a medication that is commonly prescribed for children who suffer from ADD. "Amber took Ritalin for six months and her grades improved. Her teachers were amazed. But it was still hard for her. She still forgot things. Also, it was hard for her to remember to take her medication."

Then the psychiatrist and the educational psychologist suggested that Amber be enrolled in a school that required an even higher IQ for admittance—a minimum IQ of 145. The therapists felt that the school's intellectually stimulating environment would get Amber excited about education again. "Shortly after Amber started attending this school, she met a friend there who began to sell her cocaine," Chuck recalls with a deep sigh of resignation. Amber's friend, who had an even higher IQ than she did, was intellectually sophisticated and wanted to make money.

Not surprisingly, Amber's behavior took a dramatic turn for the worse, though Chuck and Brenda didn't realize drug use was at the root of what was happening. One antic involved Amber disappearing to hang out on the streets, when she had told her mother she was spending the night with a girlfriend. Chuck, who was away at a business meeting in Washington, D.C., got a call from a frantic Brenda. "I left my meeting and flew home. We were so co-dependent, in those days, because no matter what, we stopped anything we were doing to respond to Amber, which only enabled her to do something else."

Rushing home did not stop Amber's rebellious behavior. Shortly after that incident, she was caught in the restroom at school drinking alcohol, she was taking money from her mother's purse to pay for her cocaine habit, and she became a good liar. Chuck remembers the anger he felt when he found out Amber was a drug abuser. "I was mad at her teachers, the district, the police, I thought it was the fault of the city, and I wanted to murder everybody. I never thought it was the fault of a dysfunctional family." Amber had just turned 13 when they discovered she was a heavy cocaine user. "It blew my mind. I wanted to escape, I wanted to move to Oregon. It was a depersonalizing situation. It was like looking down at some real sad people."

He and Brenda started attending group family counseling sessions at the drug treatment facility where Amber was enrolled, but at first their attitude was, "We have to participate in this? I thought they were going to fix *her*." They stuck it out, however, and "the more we went to meetings, the more we learned and began to understand that we were contributing to our daughter's dysfunction." Eventually they changed their opinion about the group parent meetings. Chuck laughs as he explains, "It got to the point where we felt lucky to be in the program and on free nights would say, 'What are we going to do tonight? What are we doing here? What are we doing home?'"

One member of the family, however, was not faring as well as the others. "Linda had always been the star, but all of the turmoil around Amber was hard on her, and her grades started to drop." Linda's grades improved, though, as she began to pay more attention to what Chuck and Brenda revealed about themselves during the parent meetings. "She started listening to what was going on at these meetings and realized that she was being controlled by demanding parents, and she learned that there was more to life than making Mom and Dad happy. Then we had two problems on our hands."

Chuck adds, "Luckily we were in a loving, supportive situation with our group and had had enough therapy so that we began to allow her the freedom that she needed to become her own person. Linda still has a lot of things to work out because of what Brenda and I laid on her, but she's getting there. She's becoming more independent and the more she does, the healthier she gets. She's got her grades up and is planning, on her own recognizance, to apply for college. It's what she wants to do. I must say I encourage her, but I don't tell her what she needs to do anymore. It's a different lifestyle, and I don't like everything about it—their rooms are both trash heaps these days, but their rooms are their own business." By adopting this attitude, Chuck has become less demanding and more tolerant, thereby allowing his daughters to learn how to make choices and live with the consequences of those choices.

Given what the family has experienced and accomplished, does Chuck anticipate a great future for his daughters? "I think Amber may have a better shot since she's more committed to the recovery process because of her history of substance abuse. Still, it's going to be really difficult for my kids *not* to have dysfunctional families, because they grew up in one. We demanded that Linda live her life according to our goals for her future. We made almost all of her decisions for her and demanded that she do exactly what we told her, so we didn't allow her to make her own mistakes. I see that over and over in myself and it's an eerie feeling—it feels as if I'm being just like my father."

Amber

Amber, 15, divides her life into two periods: before she hit, and after. Her reference to "hit" has to do with the self-destructive lifestyle she embraced while abusing alcohol and cocaine, starting when she was 12. When she describes her father, she describes him from the vantage point of how her history of substance abuse impacted his personality. "Before I hit, he was always in a good mood. If mother was angry he just tried to calm her down, but he never got angry himself. I really have some good memories of him. Something I really remember is when he used to work on his car. We used to go out to the garage and listen to the radio and talk about all kinds of things. After I hit, he was going to work more and staying there more and coming home later. My mom would get angry at that and cause a fight."

Brenda, according to Amber, was always the more volatile parent. "My mom was more stressed, more—I hate to say—hyper. While Dad was always trying to calm me or my mother down, she was always yelling." Amber also recognizes her mother's generosity, although Brenda's penchant for gift-giving caused Amber some uncomfortable moments. "She was always doing her best for me by buying me a lot of things like expensive tennis shoes. She loved to see me in things. I don't know if it was an attempt to make me how she wanted me or what, but I would feel bad when she would give me a present that I didn't like or particularly want. I was afraid it would hurt her feelings if I told her what I really felt about the present."

Whatever her parents' strengths or weaknesses, Amber considers her upbringing to have been good. "They taught me values. I really think that they brought me up well. I don't know why I started using drugs. It was not because of peer pressure. I just went up to a person and told him I wanted to buy a gram of coke and that's how it started." Amber pauses. "Maybe I started using coke because I felt bad. I got depressed all the time. I was a depressive person."

At first Amber is not sure how she became so depressive. After a moment of reflection, however, she tells a chilling tale of how she believes it all began. "It started when I was in the sixth grade. My father put a lot of pressure on me about school. I didn't feel like I was good enough for him. I always had this feeling that he would love me more if I did better, if I got first place instead of second place, if I could achieve more. Mother would yell at me and tell me that I was the most self-centered person she knew. She still does that. I felt unloved and I had all of these feelings balled up inside of me. I really felt as if I was going insane in a way. I would just sit and stare at things. I had this person in my head who would tell me what to do, would talk to me. This person would punish me and tell me to cut myself. Sometimes this person would say, 'You don't deserve shit. You're a piece of shit.' "

Too often Amber followed the advice of the "person" in her head and used a razor blade or a safety pin to carve phrases such as "Fuck Life" into her legs. She also admits to having slashed her wrist four times. Once her father caught her in the act of self-mutilation. It was the only time he ever used physical restraint to control or discipline her. "My dad has never touched me except for this one incident when I had cut my wrist and I was trying to get away from him. I hit him in the balls twice, but he wouldn't let go of my arms. Instead, he kept asking, 'Amber, what's going on here?' And he was almost crying." It was during this period that Amber began using cocaine, marijuana, and alcohol, though she says that her drug use had nothing to do with hearing the "person" because she recalls that she was not high during those moments. Her parents, however, were not so sure that there was no connection. Beyond that concern, they were terrified by all that was happening, and so they sought outside help.

"My parents took me to about nine different psychiatrists to try to fix me when I was using drugs." She experienced a turning point during her eight-month stay at Saint Joseph's Hospital in Los Angeles, a residential drug treatment facility that involves all family members in the recovery process. After being allowed to leave the facility on a pass, Amber tested positive for drugs on her return—when, she emphatically reports, she had not used any. She was punished anyway. "I was so angry about that [the punishment], I was shaking for about a week. But I got honest with a lot of my feelings after that incident, and it became a turning point for me, because I used to lie a lot about what I really felt when I first went into the Saint Joseph's program."

Amber emphasizes that it wasn't "acceptable" to feel certain emotions in her household prior to the counseling the family has received since it was discovered she was using drugs. "Being angry wasn't okay in our family. My dad used to say, 'Don't be angry. You shouldn't be angry.'" Yet Amber witnessed a number of arguments between her parents and not a little anger directed toward her—all of which left her both frightened and furious. "I got scared when my parents fought and that made me angry. I got angry when I couldn't get what I wanted. And I got scared and angry when my mother got upset and would throw things at me, like a burrito. Once she even ripped the phone out of the wall because I was talking to a boyfriend too long and didn't hang up fast enough when she told me to say goodbye."

Familial dynamics have changed for the better for all concerned since Amber entered drug treatment three years ago. "I used to hide from my parents right before I started using drugs. I would find places in the house where it was hard to locate me, and I would stare silently at things a lot. I feel much safer at home now. Before, I didn't love them. I felt like I couldn't love them. But I've learned from my experiences. I've learned that my parents have feelings, too. I've learned that if you feel angry or hurt, that's not bad, it's what you do with what you feel that makes the difference. Now I feel like my own person, rather than a clone of them."

Amber acknowledges that there is work yet to be done in the household, especially in terms of her older sister. "I've always been afraid for her because she doesn't talk, not only about her feelings but about anything." During group family counseling meetings, Linda always introduced herself by saying, "Hi, I'm Linda and I feel okay," even if the family was in the throes of a major crisis. When Amber would ask her how she was doing, Linda had a stock response: "It's cool, don't worry about it." Amber continues to feel at a loss as to how she can help Linda cope with what she believes are repressed feelings. Amber sounds worried, when she states, "I don't know what to do."

Amber also continues to examine her own behavior and isn't always happy with what she sees. "I haven't been without a boyfriend since the middle of the sixth grade, and I think it's because they tell me that I'm okay." It concerns her that she needs that outside reinforcement. And Amber still is having trouble expressing her anger. "I am passive-aggressive with my mom. I say 'okay' to her when she's trying to get me to do something I don't want to do, but then I don't do what I've agreed to do." Such behavior is a classic example of the child of a demanding parent. Still rebelling against her parents, Amber admits as well that she's involved in a cut-off-her-nose-to-spite-her-face game with her mother concerning her grades at school. "I do bad in my classwork because I know my mother really cares about it and she can't do anything about it if I don't do well." Amber realizes that she's hurting herself more than her mother in the long run, but she continues to play the game while acknowledging that she wants to stop. Overall, though, Amber is feeling better than ever about herself. "I used to wonder about who I am. Now I am beginning to know."

Linda

Seventeen-year-old Linda is shy, self-effacing, and generally does very little talking. "I get embarrassed pretty easily." She comes to life, however, when she talks about her parents and her sister. "I didn't like them [Brenda and Chuck], especially Mom [when Amber was using drugs]. I felt like I couldn't really talk to Mom. She usually didn't hear what I had to say." In spite of this criticism, Linda considers her upbringing to have been "pretty happy." What bad memories she has revolve around how

Amber got along in the household, not how she herself fared. "My mom was always getting mad at my sister. She would get mad and hit her, then feel bad about it and apologize later. She apologized a lot. It seemed to me that she would get mad at Amber more than me." Linda reflects, "Maybe Mom and Dad expected more from Amber than they did from me."

Linda was at odds with her sister, though, when she found out that Amber had become a substance abuser. "I never knew she was using any drugs. I felt pretty betrayed. Amber usually told me everything she did." Linda recalls as well that she was "more stressed" in the 10th grade because of Amber's problems.

These days, both her academic and home life are on the upswing. Linda is preparing for college; Amber, according to Linda, has become more mature; and Brenda and Chuck "don't yell at us anymore. They really aren't strict parents now. In fact, we're kind of spoiled."

Postscript

In many ways, this family fits the classic demanding parent model. Demanding parents push, prod, and pressure their children to accept the hero's role. Brenda and Chuck, for instance, insisted that Amber and Linda attend schools that catered to the brightest children in the community, even if it meant that the parents had to do the homework to ensure report cards covered with A's. Such dictatorial methods of parenting had some pretty predictable results: two children who are burdened with feelings of inadequacy because they were seldom permitted to express their own opinions and individuality, and who are acting out both door-mat and rebel personas—a classic consequence of demanding parenting.

Amber became the family scapegoat and rebel by displaying anger and frustration through her substance abuse and through her repeated acts of self-mutilation. The family's hero, Linda, also matches the description of the lost child. Although for the most part she did well in school and caused few problems, Linda is very shy, has few associates, and is alone much of the time. Moreover, as Chuck describes, "Linda has no self-respect. She doesn't attempt things that she's capable of doing." And, according to her sister, Linda will not talk about her emotional pain. Too often Linda says she's okay when it is difficult to believe that could be the case, Amber reports.

It is interesting to note too how this family deviates from the demanding parent model—a reflection of the fact that no family can be neatly categorized. Brenda's testimony, for example, seemed confusing at times. She identifies strongly with her father, though she admits that he seldom spoke to her as a child, was rarely at home because of his workaholism, and never expressed his emotions. On the other hand, Brenda did not resonate to her mother—a warm and nurturing although volatile personality. Given Brenda's description of her childhood, there appears to be no history of demanding parents in her background, although Chuck, Amber, and Linda all "testify" that Brenda was quite demanding in raising her own children. Through Brenda's eyes, Amber's rebellious behavior is inexplicable. Through Amber's eyes, her mother's behavior is unacceptable: "I would say that my mother drove me to using drugs because she yells at me a lot and I feel unloved when she does that."

If the overall report of this family is to be believed, Brenda is in denial about the nature and extent of her co-dependency. The rest of the family members, however, do not always confront Brenda with their frank opinion of her behavior. Several times during my interviews with this family, in fact, I was asked not to include certain comments about Brenda for fear it would upset her to hear what the family really felt about her. So, to that extent, there appears to be some unspoken and informal collusion among this family to publicly go along with Brenda's view of herself. Consequently, this family's recovery is uneven, held back by Brenda's denial and the family's unwillingness to openly grapple with that denial.

The most important lesson I learned from interviewing this family and the other families for this book is that parents are as much the victims of their co-dependent upbringing as are their children. Typically, mothers and fathers have grappled with many of the same issues their children are struggling to sort out. Just as Brenda did not like her mother's volatility, her daughters are unhappy with Brenda's emotional ups and downs. Just as Chuck battled with his father's demanding parenting, which he rebelled against as he grew older, so has Amber fought against her father's and mother's dictatorial behavior by using drugs and harming herself with safety pins and razors. Just as I initially turned my back on my mother's determination of what my future should hold, my son is in the process of etching out a lifestyle that only remotely resembles what I would have wanted for him.

Now that you have read this chapter, take the time to identify at least three areas of struggle you had with your parents. Ask your spouse to do the same with regard to his or her parents. Then ask yourself a tough question and prepare yourself for an honest answer: How have you related to your children around these same issues?

CHAPTER 4

THE CRITICAL PARENT

I am very sensitive to criticism, yet I have chosen to spend a good portion of my life surrounded by judgmental people who are quick to criticize me. Only recently did I figure out why: I attract people who excessively point out my weaknesses because I was routinely criticized as a child; so it is a familiar experience, and there is comfort in familiarity.

Both Mother and Father were critical parents, but had very different styles. Mother was overtly critical. Father was critical, but in a subtle way. My sister still cringes as she recalls an example of my mother's more direct approach: "Mom would say to me, 'You're such a pretty child, but you have such a terrible personality.'" My father, however, would read one of my school essays and flatly state, "Barbara didn't write that." The implication was that the essay was so good that I could not have written it, but my father would never straightforwardly own up to that belief. I was left feeling powerless during these encounters and believed there was very little I could do that was right, although I strived to prove my parents and others wrong in the years to come.

So I grew up living a contradiction. On the one hand, I hated to be criticized. Still, I was quite comfortable existing within a judgmental environment because I was so accustomed to criticism. Consequently, in choosing my first two husbands, I chose men who picked up where my parents left off—both spouses often expressed negative opinions about me. My first husband told me that I was unattractive and had better stay with him because no one else would want me. My second husband was embarrassed by the fact that I had been married before and had a child from that marriage, so he repeatedly reminded me of how many bad choices I had made prior to marrying him.

As I ventured out professionally, I was drawn to the same kind of relationships. For example, I seemed inevitably prone to work for bosses who found fault with my work no matter how highly I was praised by all others around me. I tended to look over my shoulder wondering when or where the next blow would fall. Even my posture was affected by my expectations of criticism from my employers and from my parents—I developed a way of walking with my shoulders perpetually hunched in a guarded position. But until very recently, I would not walk away from ever-critical individuals. To the contrary, I virtually would embrace them.

It was not the bad treatment I received from others, however, that jogged my awareness of what it meant to be raised by critical parents. Instead, I began to examine this co-dependent pattern when I finally realized what I was doing to my current spouse and my son. I was a very critical wife and mother. During a vacation in Europe, I discovered how critical of my husband I could be. He had never been to London and was a little disoriented by the difference in culture, climate (we live in Southern California), and currency. I became extremely impatient and began to disparage him at virtually every opportunity. "Why are you so nervous?" I asked. "Do you mean you've never been on a subway? How could you have lived so long and not have ridden on a subway?" Fortunately for my husband and myself, I quickly took note of what I was doing and stopped. But it is a behavior that I must constantly monitor.

Self-discovery of how critical I can be with my 22-year-old son took place over the telephone. He had decided to become serious with his girlfriend, and I didn't like that decision. She was not the young lady I would have chosen for him. When my more direct efforts to convey my opinions did not achieve the desired effect, I tried a more subtle approach. I attempted to diminish her in his eyes by asking questions about her that I knew could only be answered in the negative. When that tactic failed, I went for the jugular by using an insidious line of questioning that was more statement than query: "Why don't I believe that you're going to be faithful to this girl for the rest of your life?" I was mortified to hear myself—I sounded just like my parents, which caused me to pay more attention to my son's language. And much to my chagrin, as I listened to him in subsequent conversations, I realized that my son sounded just like me.

"YOU DON'T DO ANYTHING RIGHT"

Classically critical parents generally are demanding in the extreme. They are negative, judgmental people who use criticism to control their children so that their sons and daughters will become compliant and do whatever they are told. Such parents find fault with most every action of their children. Behind this critical and controlling facade, however, are parents who are dissatisfied with themselves because they too were criticized as children and believed what their parents said. So these mothers and fathers give out the same message to their children: "You don't do anything right."

Ironically, though critical parents feel like failures, they also are perfectionists. Their perfectionism is a tool they use in an attempt to obtain approval from their parents. In other words, if they can produce super-achieving children, they will have proven to their parents their own value. So they push and castigate their sons and daughters to reach impossible goals, and then assail them when they fail. Perfectionism, then, becomes a double-edged sword, a tool that is used to go after what cannot be attained. Thus, critical parents are by definition setting their children and themselves up to fail, which ultimately proves the legacy: they and their offspring *can't* do anything right.

Some critical parents play out the lose-lose game in a distinctly different manner, although the results are the same—both parent and child believe they are failures. These parents are judgmental about others in order to feel good about themselves. They like to prove that they are right and everyone else is wrong. They put down their children because they see them as competition. Such mothers and fathers live in perpetual fear that their children may show them up—may know more about something than they do, for example, or look more attractive. So they openly and deliberately sabotage their children's success by undermining their self-confidence. Basically, these parents have a very fragile sense of superiority. Underneath it all, they really don't like themselves because they feel there is no way to live up to their own parents' expectations. They feel like losers since they cannot entirely shield themselves from their perceived competition (their children), and the children feel like losers living under a constant parental bombardment of negativity.

Perfectionism leads critical parents to focus a great deal of energy and resources on keeping secrets. These parents and their children are quite concerned with their image and they want to look good to others and to themselves at almost any cost. To that end, they are emotionally withdrawn and generally inaccessible, personifying the three tenets of dysfunctional family life mentioned in Chapter 2: don't talk, don't feel, don't trust. Past and present blots or potential blots on the perfectionist image of these families are kept in the background by denial. The rule (implicit or explicit) is that such matters must not be discussed or acknowledged. A by-product of such suppression in these families is fear and distrust

because of a prevailing uncertainty: will the pact to keep the family secrets be honored?

My father was a compulsive gambler. All of us children knew this but
rarely talked about it. During my childhood I even lost a good friend
because I was admonished to keep the family skeleton in the closet. One
summer my father had opted not to pay the water bill in favor of meeting
his obligations with loan sharks. A girlfriend of mine, whose parents had
been very generous with me over the previous year, asked to spend a
weekend with me because her parents were going out of town. I wanted
to tell my friend the truth as to why she could not stay at our house (we
didn't have any running water), but my mother insisted that I not respond
to her entreaties to spend the night. My friend and her parents were hurt
by the apparent snub and cut me off from that moment forward.

Like me, children of critical parents become angry and resentful and
afraid of risking failure because of the lose-lose situation they find themselves in. Virtually all of these children spend a lifetime trying to prove
their worth to their parents in a variety of ways, yet they all remain wary
of making mistakes. Even though many of them are superachievers, their
typical modus operandi is to attempt only what they believe they can do
well. Such children may find an excuse to bail out of a project or relationship if it looks like their chances to succeed are going downhill. For example, I tend to overcommit myself and then procrastinate as a hedge
against failure. If I don't end up with a good product, I blame it on my
workload and lack of time to properly complete the task. If I pull off the
impossible, I get to pat myself on the back and temporarily, at least, believe in my bionic status. Thus I prove that I am a valuable person and that
I can do something right. In my world, then, I am ostensibly protected
from failure. I am still left in a lose-lose situation, though, because on
some level I believe that my success is contrived. As a child of critical
parents, I don't feel really good for very long about whatever miracle I
have pulled off. Instead, I often feel as if I am a phony, like the Wizard of
Oz waiting to be found out. Basically, no matter how well such children
do, no matter what gains they make, they still hear and believe the criticism delivered by their parents.

BECOMING AWARE

These days, my critical parent is inside my head. My father is dead,
and over the years my mother has genuinely changed. She's not nearly as
critical as she once was. Yet, I struggle with an extremely self-critical
character. There are times when I am even harder on myself than my

mother ever was. In essence, I learned all too well from my parents how to tear myself down. And my son has learned the very same lesson from me. When he makes a mistake, if I start to chide him for his error in judgment, he almost always stops me to say, "Mom, don't you think I know what you're telling me? Don't you realize that I've already told myself everything you're saying and more?" Typically, I am stopped short by his response, because the critical script I am reciting to him is bad enough. It is quite disheartening at such moments to imagine that what he is telling himself is worse than my commentary. So I am trying to learn to listen carefully to myself and to my son, and start the process of reprogramming the negative, judgmental messages both of us have carried inside our heads many for many years.

To help you determine whether your language falls into the critical parent category, I have selected a few examples of the type of statements such mothers and fathers routinely make to their children. The original list was compiled by teachers from the Hacienda–La Puente (California) School District.

- "What were you thinking of when you did that?"
- "You dummy!"
- "I can't believe you did that."
- "You look terrible. Go change."
- "You never do anything right."
- "I can't believe you did that again when I told you not to."
- "Just what do you think you are doing?"
- "You really didn't want to do that, did you?"
- "You're just like your father."
- "Sit up straight, stop biting your nails..."

Critical parents chip away at their children's self-confidence by setting up scenarios to ensure that their offspring lose face and faith in their self-worth. They find ways to continually remind their children of how stupid or unattractive or untalented they are. On the face of it, these parents believe that what they are saying about their sons and daughters is true and in the best interest of their children. They tend to have so much confidence in themselves that they appear self-righteous. In truth, these parents are hiding behind their self-righteousness to obscure how poorly they really feel about themselves. Consequently, these parents show very little emotion because they fear that their secret will be exposed if they let anyone—especially their children—get too close.

Margo, the daughter whose sole testimony comprises this chapter's family profile, provides an extreme example of the distance imposed by critical parents. Margo, 42, has not seen or spoken to her mother in approximately 23 years—at her mother's request and after years of conflict based on her mother's belief that Margo was her arch competitor. It appears that Margo's mother felt threatened by her daughter's blond beauty, especially after Margo's father died and her mother started dating men who were near her daughter's age. Because of the estranged relations between these two women, Margo does not know the whereabouts of her mother, so the parent could not be interviewed for this book.

The classic child of a critical parent, Margo has been a workaholic superachiever who once reached the top ranks of corporate America. Still, she confesses that she was unhappy much of that time and wishes she could believe that her parents loved her. Married twice, Margo is currently divorced. She says that she wants to marry again but has a recent history of choosing men who mistreat her in a variety of ways—from pretending to be monogamous to deliberately keeping her at bay emotionally (and sometimes physically) while leading her on. Margo typically breaks up with these men after a short period of time so that she gets to reject them before they reject her—a pattern her therapist says is linked to her critical upbringing. The co-dependent dynamics of this family profile are particularly subtle. Rather than criticize Margo directly, her mother found a myriad of ways to set Margo up to be criticized, ridiculed, and ostracized by others—especially by her father, younger sister, and teenage peers.

Margo's sister is a drug abuser to whom she has not spoken in about four years, after "a big fight on the telephone when I asked her to give me Mother's address and she refused because she said Mother would be furious with her if she did." Her sister hung up on her. Margo does not know where her sister lives now, so she has no way of contacting her or their mother.

Very introspective, Margo has thought a great deal over the years about her own psyche and her relationship with her parents. Although she is willing to talk about her experiences and what she has learned, she was nervous throughout her testimony and wanted her name changed here. Even assurances of anonymity didn't leave her entirely comfortable; there were moments when she questioned whether people should know certain things about her history. Margo reluctantly admits that she worries about her image, about what other people will think of her—a legacy of her critical past.

FAMILY PROFILE:

Margo

Margo wears a creased brow nearly as often as a broad smile. She is a worrier. Margo worries about finding her ideal mate; her biological clock regarding childbirth; her weight, though she is slender; the tiny lines around her eyes that are beginning to emerge, though she is youthful looking; and, most of all, she is often fearful of whether family, friends, or lovers are preparing to reject her. "My greatest fear is, and always has been, the fear of rejection. Yet, if I'm not rejected, I reject first." Margo reports with much regret that she has walked away from "enough people who have played an emotionally significant role in my life to fill up a ballroom." She is better than she would like to be at disposing of relationships, because "it's what I was taught by my parents." Margo was raised by two very critical parents who disapproved of most of her actions and then ignored her as a form of punishment.

About four years ago, Margo experienced what she calls her "metanoia," a change of heart that led to a religious conversion to Catholicism. Her newfound spiritual values coupled with therapy have helped her to recognize the co-dependent patterns of behavior that plague her from her critical upbringing. At one time she thought she had forgiven her parents, but today she admits that she is still angry with them both—an emotion she wants to shake. But, she says, "When I'm feeling as if I want to reject someone, it's just like stepping up to my father and having him turn his face away. And that's a feeling I don't want to experience, and rejecting good friends out of hand is an experience I don't want to keep repeating."

"My mother was beautiful, truly a beautiful woman," Margo recalls. "She was what I wish I looked like now. So this was a woman who had no need of being insecure, on the face of it." Yet, Margo's mother was extremely competitive with her daughter as to who would be the best looking in their household, especially as Margo entered her teen years. It appears that her mother began an all-out campaign to ensure that Margo would not win the competition. "When I was 12 to 14, the girls in school were very clothes conscious, very fashion conscious. They had pretty little shoes, pretty pumps, and just the right lipstick and hairdo. If you dressed accordingly, you were in the in-crowd. If you didn't, you were in the out-crowd. Well, it seems like my mother did everything she could to make sure I was in the out-crowd."

Margo had to wear her dresses three days in a row, even though money was not an issue in her middle-class family. "Instead, it looks as though my mother was trying to make sure that I didn't fit in. If I ever complained she would say, 'That's not an issue. If you look different, that's great. It builds character.' And the dresses she wanted me to wear looked like something out of the 'Little House on the Prairie' television show. My mother also decided that she wanted me to have nice, strong ankles, so she took me to an orthopedic shoes place to buy orthopedic oxfords. Everybody else at my high school was wearing shoes with a one-inch heel, almost like the shoes that are popular today—and I would be wearing these great big brown oxfords. It looked like a man's shoe."

She also was forced by her mother to wear her hair in an unattractive style, and Margo's rebellion around this issue led to a six-month expulsion, of sorts, from the family. "Mother kept my hair cut about one inch long all over. I worked my hair into what was called a ducktail style, but the popular style was a longish, curled bouffant. When I was almost 14, my mother, who set her hair every night in rollers because in those days hot rollers did not exist, just came into my room one night as I was beginning to set my hair and said, 'You may not set your hair anymore.' And I said, 'Why not?' And she said, 'It's unhealthy for you. It is unhealthy for you to go to bed in rollers and to sleep on rollers.' Now, remember, my mother was going to bed every night with a head full of rollers.

"My hair, at the time, was short, very thick, naturally curly and unruly. So I needed the rollers just to kind of smooth it out. Otherwise, it would be really ugly looking. There was no way that I could just go to bed and wake up and do my hair because there weren't even blow dryers then. You either slept on rollers or you got up in the morning, set your hair, and sat under a hair dyer, which I didn't own. So my mother came in and told me I couldn't set my hair anymore. When I pleaded and begged, I got the standard, 'Don't argue with me' from my mother. Well, I panicked. I freaked, because I thought, 'My God, there is no way that I can wake up in the morning and go to school with my hair sticking out in all directions.'

"So about two in the morning, I sat up in bed and, as stealthily as I could, started setting my hair in rollers, in the dark, thinking a couple of hours in rollers would at least smooth it somewhat. But what happened next was weird. It was like my mother knew what I was doing, because she came flying into the bedroom the first time I tried to sneak and roll my hair. She comes in, throws on the light switch, and acts as though I was caught robbing a bank, because she takes the rollers away from me, swears at me for disobeying her, and tells me that this will be dealt with tomorrow. With that, she took my rollers and left. When my father got home the next night, I remember coming from my bedroom out to the living room to kiss my father hello. But, this day, the day after the roller episode, my father turned his face away. He didn't say anything, he just turned his face away as though to say, 'I don't want you to kiss me.' So I knew mother had told him about the rollers and he was angry."

Margo's father remained angry for the next six months. "It was as though I had died. I had to eat out in the kitchen, while they ate in the dining room. He didn't speak to me at Christmas. That whole day it was like I was dead. My younger sister loved it, because it was like she was the only child. She got to sit in the dining room for family meals, and on weekends they would do things together, but I was not to be included. It was horrible—talk about feeling like the loner. And the only reason that he made up with me was because he was diagnosed with terminal leukemia. But, at the time, I didn't know he had leukemia and that he was dying, I just knew that he had vicious headaches. That's why he made up with me. Otherwise, that ostracism would have gone on forever."

The ostracism stopped, but the bad treatment Margo received during her childhood continued even after her father's death. "He died at the beginning of my senior year in high school, and right after that my mother started dating again, and she started dating men in their early 20s. She was 37 when my dad died, I was 17, and there was one man that she dated who was 22. When he would come over to pick her up, I never saw him. I just heard him, because I had to stay in my bedroom since she didn't want me to meet him. Mother was jealous and envious of me, but I would have to say that I was not an attractive kid. I probably could have been attractive with a mother who said, 'Let's make sure your hair is as pretty as it can be; and, here, you can wear a little pink lipstick and wear cute clothes.' But anyway, she was dating younger men and keeping me under wraps. And then when I graduated from high school—my mother was not college educated, my father had been, but not my mother—she didn't want me going to college."

Margo abided by her mother's wishes and went to work. Shortly thereafter, she met the man who was to become her first husband. All went well in the beginning. Her mother seemed to like Margo's new male friend, so much so that she accepted an invitation for her and Margo to spend a weekend in Las Vegas at his expense. "Mother had a rip-roaring time. And when I say rip-roaring, boy, did I see a different side of my mother. He took us to this big Las Vegas show, and my mother, who was ostensibly the biggest prude in the world, got real stiff when the topless dancers came out. But after a few drinks, she loosened up and was ready to join them on the stage. My boyfriend was really nice to both of us. He really took good care of us during this outing. When we got back, I remember sitting with Mother in the living room and she was setting her hair and all of a sudden she makes a pronouncement that I cannot see my boyfriend anymore.

"I was absolutely incredulous. Here we'd had this wonderful time. He'd been a perfect gentleman. I thought, 'What could possibly have prompted this?' Well, Mother said that my boyfriend, who was Persian, looked like a Negro. I wished he looked like Harry Belafonte or some great-looking black man. But he didn't. There was no way you would confuse him with being black. Absolutely none. But mother said, 'He looks like a Negro and when we were in Las Vegas and we were sitting there at dinner, there were people over at the other tables and they were staring at us, and they would stare at him and stare at us, and I don't want you with someone who looks like a Negro.' "

Margo, then 17, argued in support of her boyfriend. She said she was not going to stop seeing him. Her mother was not swayed. "After a while, what Mother said was, 'Okay. You've made your choice. I am leaving this house.' And she packed her bags and left. My sister, who is fours years younger, became unglued. We were thinking that Mother was never coming back." She stayed away for four days, never communicating with either of her daughters. "We were able to function. I continued to work and my sister went to school. But since I didn't know how to drive, I would catch the bus to get to work and my boyfriend would drive me home at night. On the fourth day, I had a premonition. When my boyfriend drove up my driveway, I told him, 'Don't leave. Please stay here.' I felt something was wrong. I got up to the front door and started to put my key into the front door and it flew open. My mother was inside and handed me a suitcase and said, 'You don't live here any more. You have made your choice to continue to see this man. You do not live here anymore. You can come and get your things on the weekend.' With that declaration, my mother slammed the door in my face. Well, talk about hysterical. I went absolutely berserk." Once Margo retrieved her belongings, she never saw or spoke to her mother again.

Years later, Margo found out in talks with her sister that once she had left, her sister became the focus of their mother's jealousy and ill treatment. Her mother kicked her sister out of the family home when she was still in high school. Consequently, her sister never went back to get her diploma and ended up a drug abuser. Through reports from her sister, Margo discovered that her mother remarried, but she doesn't know if she is still married. Her mother has refused to talk to her and, these days, Margo doesn't know where her sister resides. "I tried to communicate with Mother over the years. My boyfriend who became my first husband tried to communicate with her. We sent her roses, we tried to call her, but she would never talk to me. It was like I had just died."

The genesis of Margo's acrimonious relationship with her sister is rooted in their unhealthy family life. During the four years, for example, that her younger sister remained at home after Margo's ouster, Margo was blocked by her mother from contact with her sibling. Years passed, and Margo finally tracked down her sister through a friend, but "by the time I did, my sister was on drugs. She subsequently married a man who physically beat her, and in addition to using drugs she became an alcoholic. She dropped out of my life for years. I didn't know where she worked, none of her friends knew where she was living, and her phone was disconnected. Then one day, out of the blue, I got a phone call from her. And it was in that phone call that she said she knew where Mother was. She said she knew Mother's phone number, but she told me, 'I can't give it to you. Mother says that she wants no contact with you, that you went with that man who looked like a Negro, and she doesn't want to have anything to do with you anymore. So if you want to find her, get yourself a private detective.' I got angry. There were words. My sister hung up and I didn't have a phone number to get back to her, and I haven't heard from her since—and that's been five years."

It has been virtually impossible for Margo to come by clues as to what type of childhood her mother had. She does know there were long stretches of time when her mother refused to talk to her own mother and sister. "When I was growing up, my grandmother was out of my life for a year and a half at various points, because she and Mother weren't speaking. [Mother] also didn't speak to my aunt, her oldest sister, from time to time, so I didn't see much of my aunt when I was growing up." As an adult, Margo learned from some of her father's relatives that her mother would mistreat them when they came to visit, and that they wrote off her mother as being incredibly insecure. They believed Margo's mother simply wanted to cut off her husband from his family—and apparently succeeded.

Margo knows a little more about her father's childhood, when he was criticized through ridicule. "He was raised very strictly in a very affluent family. His family dressed formally for dinner. And one time when he was seven years old, he wet his bed, and his father dressed him in a girl's christening gown and put a bonnet on his head and made him stand outside of the car on its running board, while the car was driven around town for everyone to see."

She learned something revealing about both of her parents when she became sick with pneumonia at 21 and went to the same doctor who had treated her father for cancer. "I found out so much about my parents from him. He said that emotionally, they were like two children. Of course, I never saw my father as childlike, but this doctor said that from the time he told them my father was dying of leukemia, they went into a never-never land. It wasn't a 'we will lick this through faith' kind of feeling. It was more like two little children holding hands, running through the meadow, refusing to face up to what was happening in terms of any type of planning. The doctor told them that my father was going to die, and it was as though he had said, 'You're going to the post office tomorrow.' "

So her parents did not prepare themselves or their children. "My sister and I had no idea that he was dying. None. In fact, I resented spending so much time at the hospital—which I now feel guilty about—but I didn't know he was dying. On the day that he died, his sister was visiting, and my mother told me that my father's last words were, 'The two women I love the most in the world are standing with me here right now.' Not 'tell my daughters I love them,' but the two women he loved the most were his sister and his wife."

Given Margo's history, her father's deathbed pronouncement is not all that surprising. Indeed, one particular daily ritual epitomized the second-class role that underscored Margo's and her sister's relationship with their parents. "Mom would prepare for hours for dad's return home from work. She would spend about three hours getting ready for him. She would place frozen daiquiris in the freezer, she would take a long perfumed bubble bath, wear a long hostess dress, fix her hair and her makeup every business day. And when he would get home, she would meet him with the frozen daiquiris and then they would go out into our tropical garden by the swimming pool and sit for about two hours. My sister and I were permitted to say hello and kiss Father on the cheek—and that's it. We were not allowed to disturb Mother and Father until dinner. They would talk over whatever they talked about, but we were not included. In the summer months, they were outside. In winter months, they would do this in the living room, and they closed off the hall to the bedrooms, so that my sister and I would be in our bedroom with the hallway door closed, and they'd be in the living room."

These days, Margo recognizes that she was hurt in a number of significant ways by the events and rituals that took place during her childhood. "I went through two marriages and I couldn't tell you what love is, because I wasn't taught to love. I was taught how to criticize, punish, and reject." She adds, "I was raised on conditional love and I practiced conditional love. I was raised without any religion, without any moral underpinning, so that when things weren't working out in my marriages I left, I rejected my spouses as I was rejected by my parents as a child and young adult." Despite the pain and anger that show on Margo's face as she describes her past, there resides within her a desire to make it better between her mother and herself. There is a wistfulness in her voice as she states, "I do wish, from the space where I am now, I could relate to my mother. She was critical of me because she was neurotically insecure. And my father was rejecting and unloving, and my mother fed on that out of her insecurity, but I still wish I could relate to my mother."

Postscript

Margo's parents were classically critical in a less than obvious manner —they used rejection as an insidious way of making their daughter feel insecure and thus question her worthiness. To justify their ostracism, she was subtly encouraged to believe that there was something wrong with her. Subtle tactics were employed as well to ridicule Margo. Instead of openly criticizing her oldest child, Margo's mother would orchestrate situations and circumstances to subject her child to ridicule at the hands of others. Demanding that Margo wear the same out-of-style dress three days in a row virtually ensured that her classmates made fun of her. Cutting Margo's hair unfashionably and refusing to allow her to use rollers guaranteed that Margo would have difficulty socializing with her teenage peers. Prodding her husband to stop speaking to Margo and to thus pretend she did not exist was a punishment designed to convince Margo that she was an outcast for good reasons.

Margo's adaptation to her upbringing mimics her parents' behavior in a lot of ways. Her way of punishing spouses, friends, and colleagues is to cut them out of her life if they displease her in the slightest way. Margo, like her mother, worries a lot about the maintenance of her beauty. She applies lipstick and other makeup as carefully when she is going to an exercise session as when she is going out on a date—she is always picture perfect. Indeed, Margo is a perfectionist, a classic symptom of a child of a critical parent.

Underneath it all, Margo's obsession with her beauty and her proclivity to reject others before they reject her are ways of protecting herself from failure, an attempt to prove to herself that she is a success and thus a worthy human being, a person who deserves to be loved. As is typical of children of critical parents, Margo is full of conflict. She wants to do well with her life, to feel okay about herself and gain her parents' approval, even though she has been conditioned by her mother and father to fail. Consequently, Margo simultaneously embraces two goals: she wants to be a success and she ultimately wants to become a failure.

Margo is struggling with her recovery and has made some gains. She is no longer in denial as to how she has thus far run her life, for instance. But she still finds it difficult to change her behavior, and she wonders if it would be easier if she had a relationship with her mother and could at least talk to her about her conflicts.

The lesson I learned from this family profile and my own critical upbringing was how much every word and every action counts when it comes to raising a child, and how easy it is for childhood incidents to become pivotal affairs in the mind of a child. Much of what I have recounted about how I was raised, incidents that sear my memory to this day, are things my mother doesn't remember. When my son was about 13 and sat down with me to review my history of poor parenting, he told me vividly about events I had little recall of. If Margo's father were still alive, it would not surprise me if he discounted the effect his period of ostracism had on his elder daughter, or even forgot the incident had taken place.

Do you have any idea what your child believes are the really significant events that have transpired between the two of you? Take the time to jog your memory by first making a list of at least five pivotal incidents or verbal exchanges in your own childhood that had a resounding impact on you. Then make a similar list of at least five encounters from your and your child's past as you believe your child might have viewed the incidents. As you try to look through your child's eyes, are you surprised by what you see?

CHAPTER 5

THE OVERPROTECTIVE PARENT

Two of the three men I married were the sons of overprotective parents. In retrospect, I realize that this pattern was no accident. In both of these marriages I needed to play the co-dependent role of the overprotective mother-wife, so I subconsciously sought out the type of man who had been especially shielded by his mother from carrying out many of the basic chores and responsibilities of day-to-day life.

My second husband was allowed to leave his clothes on the floor no matter whether he was in his own room or the kitchen. He was not expected to cook any of his own meals. His mother routinely provided him with money for all manner of expenditures—as a little boy and as a man in his early thirties. Ironically, his mother extolled the virtues of moderate spending, except as it pertained to her son. As my former husband grew older and moved out on his own, his mother cooked for him almost every night and shopped for items she determined he needed in his apartment. Indeed, she made many of his decisions for him, as she had done when he was a child. Her rationale for being so involved in her son's affairs was that he needed her decision-making abilities in order not to ruin his life.

My third and current husband's overprotective upbringing was similar in that he also received a lot of attention, special care, and financial support from his mother well into adult life—in fact, well into his forties. When he separated from his first wife, for instance, my husband did not initially support his three-year-old son—his mother took over that responsibility. When my husband spent a substantial inheritance in three years and was virtually penniless at 48, his mother "loaned" him money to pay his debts.

Neither of these men entered adulthood knowing how to be an autonomous, responsible person. Neither man felt confident handling the ordinary trials and tribulations of life, since they had had very little experience taking care of themselves. Both men were passive-aggressive types—low-key, quiet, and willing to let the women in their lives pick up where their overprotective mothers had left off. Indeed, I reveled in that co-dependent opportunity to control my husbands' lives.

Once, for example, my second husband literally collapsed in tears when someone broke into his automobile, shattering a window and stealing the car radio. For him, our "bad luck" was too big a burden to bear, so I gladly stepped in to make all of the necessary calls to law enforcement officials, our insurance company and a repair shop.

Early in my current marriage I discovered that my husband did not always make a connection between what he earned and how much he could afford to spend. When a bill came due for a financial obligation that was beyond his ability to pay, often he assumed that I would either "loan" him money or use our savings to cover the expense. And, in the beginning of our marriage, he was right; I did agree to such terms and, in effect, came to his rescue.

Nowadays, both of these men are in recovery and are accepting responsibility for their lives. I, too, am learning how not to crave the co-dependent chance to control others. Also, as I learn more about what motivated me to behave in ways that were similar to my overprotective mothers-in-law, I have a better understanding of why these parents behaved as they did.

"YOU CAN'T DO IT, AT LEAST NOT BY YOURSELF"

In the classic overprotective parent model, parents give the message to their children, "You can't do it, at least not by yourself." Overprotective parents believe it is necessary to manage every aspect of their children's lives. Children of such smothering parents seldom are allowed to make their own decisions about anything, even the most mundane detail. These children end up believing that they are incompetent, or they develop a devil-may-care attitude about life and become prima donnas of the first order.

Children who feel incompetent don't have faith in themselves and are averse to taking risks, reluctant to tread unknown territory. These children spend a lot of time avoiding conflict and challenge. Often they say, "I don't know how" or "I can't do it," without trying to tackle the problem. My current husband used to invest quite a bit of energy and imagination conjuring up reasons why a prospective employer shouldn't hire him. By the time he'd finished contemplating his version of what was likely to take place, he would have convinced himself not to apply for the job.

Children who adopt a devil-may-care persona, on the other hand, tend to lead reckless, irresponsible lives because they expect their parents to clean up the messes they make. When my second marriage came to an end, for example, my former husband requested and received $8,000 from his parents to pay off his debts and buy a plane ticket to travel 3,000 miles to move back in with them—rent free. These children are prone to being devious and manipulative. They believe they are entitled to whatever they want, no matter what is at stake for their parents and others.

Overprotective parents deny their children the opportunity to become mature, responsible adults, similar to what the demanding parent does. The difference is that overprotective parents tend to control their children's lives through guilt rather than force, through covert means rather than overt demands. They use acts of self-sacrifice and purchases of material goods to gain compliance from their children. My second husband's mother fell back on the ultimate in self-sacrifice by regularly reminding him how she had jeopardized her life by choosing not to abort him during a difficult, life-threatening pregnancy. Over and over again she used this reminder to exact the behavior she desired from her son. When that approach didn't work, she took to her sickbed until her son capitulated because of his guilt.

Overprotective parents are often viewed with admiration by others or considered superior because they are generous to a fault. Nothing is too good for their children, who get anything and everything the parents can afford. In fact, some overprotective parents go into debt to ensure that their children's material desires are met, whether or not such purchases are prudent. Often these parents are trying to provide their offspring with the love, attention and material objects they themselves did not receive as children.

By looking at my own history and that of my mothers-in-law, I discovered some other reasons why overprotective parents behave the way they do. In raising my son, I was a demanding parent, at times a critical parent, and primarily a disengaging parent who as a workaholic was often too busy to spend time with my child. I was not an overprotective mother, although that was a parenting model I admired. I believed that overprotective parents who doted on their children were showing, in a most healthy manner, how much they loved their offspring. I envied them because I believed I wasn't capable of such an effusive demonstration of love, given my emotional response to my son's birth.

When my son was born I experienced postpartum depression and didn't feel a great deal of warmth toward my infant. At 16, estranged from my family for having gotten pregnant and married so early to a 19-year-old who didn't know any more than I did about a mother's potential for depression after delivering a child, I erroneously believed myself to be an unnatural mother who couldn't love her beautiful baby boy. I was afraid and for a long time silently condemned myself for my depression. I also carried around a lot of guilt that I tried to bury as time passed. When I remarried, though, for the second and third times, I initially saw the marriages as an opportunity to do for my husbands what I had not done for my son. So I became an overprotective mother-wife.

As my current husband recounts, his mother's overprotectiveness was rooted in her fear of losing yet another person she loved. Her husband had revealed himself to be homosexual within the first year or so of their marriage. For approximately 12 years following this revelation, she and her husband fashioned a marriage that allowed him to spend summers in San Francisco instead of at their home in Austin, Texas. This arrangement essentially terminated their conjugal sex life. Because of the life my husband's mother had chosen to live, she felt victimized, abandoned, and alone. As a result, she began to focus all of her available time, resources, and attention on her son.

My second husband's mother patterned her overprotective behavior after her own upbringing. Her mother had married an older widower. Though this man had several children from his previous marriage, my mother-in-law became the youngest of her father's flock and the most cherished. She was pampered and inculcated with the belief that she was special. Additionally, her family was matriarchal, so her mother saw to it that her daughter received more than her stepchildren. As the favored daughter became an adult, her mother exercised control by never letting the young woman forget how much her mother had done for her in the past and by reminding her at every turn how her disobedience could cause her aging mother's death. In essence, my husband's mother was manipulated by her mother in much the same way that she eventually came to manipulate her son.

BECOMING AWARE

Overprotective parents have a language of their own that is more subtle and less obvious in its deleterious effects than some of the other co-dependent parenting models. Becoming aware, then, of how you might be hurting your child can be difficult. To help you listen to yourself with a more informed ear, I have again selected quotes from a list developed by the teachers from the Hacienda–La Puente (California) School District who specialize in effective parenting courses.

- "You'd better let me help you."
- "It's none of your business."
- "It's just for us to worry about."
- "Do you think you are ready for that?"
- "You'd better not move ahead without asking me first."
- "I'll do that for you."
- "I am afraid you are going to get hurt."

In other words, overprotective parents control their children by covertly convincing their sons and daughters that they don't know how to take care of themselves; by shutting their children out of many decision-making processes, thus establishing a separation between themselves and their children based in part on inappropriate secrets they keep from their offspring; and by using guilt and fear to oversee their children's behavior.

The family profile for this chapter represents a classic example of overprotective parenting, though this approach to child rearing was imposed on only one of the family's three children—the youngest boy, Josh. The two older boys were raised differently by parents Mary and Bud. According to Mary, "I was much more demanding of my two oldest boys, Michael and Danny. So when Josh came along, I decided that I needed to lighten up, that maybe I had been too hard on the older boys. We went too far, though, and Josh has been the loser as a result."

FAMILY PROFILE:

Mary, Bud, Josh, and Michael

Mary, like the rest of her family, wasn't always forthcoming. Mary, apparently the chief spokesperson for this family, made herself more available to be interviewed for this book than did the other members. But she represents a number of contrasts from the rest of the family. For example, Mary, who has spent a lot of time in therapy and appears to be more open than the others, was the only family member who asked that her real first name be changed to protect her identity. Bud, described by Mary as a workaholic, quickly but pleasantly refused to be interviewed. He was too busy, he said, although he reassured me that "it's something I really wouldn't mind doing." Josh, the product of Mary's and Bud's overprotective parenting, agreed to be interviewed and then failed to show up for several scheduled interview appointments, so I did not have an opportunity to get his perspective. Michael, the eldest son, provided conflicting testimony at times, especially when he was called upon to discuss his feelings. The middle son, Danny, died a few years ago in a bicycle accident. He is rarely referred to by either Mary or Michael.

Despite these contradictions, it is apparent that this family has worked hard to attain some measure of recovery from co-dependent behaviors. Mary, who recently divorced Bud, is proud that for the first time in her life she is learning to take care of herself, to overcome her own legacy of overprotective parenting, a legacy she has passed along to her youngest son. Josh, 21, who was once caught selling drugs and then forced to attend a therapeutic boarding school by his parents, is now employed at a job that offers great potential. Michael, 30, who by his own admission has patterned his life after his workaholic father, entered therapy when he divorced a couple of years ago and is learning to be less compulsive about his employment and less overprotective of the women in his life.

Mary

Mary, 54, is petite, lively, and labels herself a "rambler" in terms of her talking pattern. She recalls how disapproving Bud was of the way she handled conversations and how she allowed herself to be bullied and bothered by his opinions. Now she is much more self-accepting and is eager to talk about what has happened to her—the end of her marriage, her overprotective relationship with her parents, the way she raised her own children, and her process of recovery. A former housewife who is on her own after having been married for a little over 30 years, Mary is still sorting out her life, and one gets the feeling that she is helped by the presence of a listener.

Mary admits that she was a demanding parent with her two older sons and an overprotective parent with Josh. She is quick to recount how everyone in the family contributed to his becoming spoiled and how the pampering led to Josh's "obnoxiousness." Today, she believes that Josh is on a solid road to recovery, but the journey is not without problems—particularly between herself and Josh. Recently the two of them had a fight that involved verbal abuse from Josh, a situation that Mary is no longer willing to put up with. Yet, within a few days she had broken her vow not to call him first to make up. And she confesses it made her feel good to detect in Josh's voice a happiness to hear from her. Mary lives in a beach town in Southern California. She is currently unemployed and living on the proceeds of her divorce. Though she is concerned about how she is going to make it relying solely on her ability to support herself, Mary is basically pleased with her progress since her divorce. "I am only now growing up. And while it's painful sometimes, I'm glad I decided to accept responsibility for my own life."

Mary was a 2½-pound baby, and she believes that precarious start in life gave rise to her parents' overprotectiveness. "My parents were afraid of losing me, and my mother couldn't have any more children, so I had a very good upbringing by standards of being loved. But I was so loved that I was overprotected. My parents didn't really allow me any independence or freedom or ability to think for myself for fear that I would make some kind of mistake and they'd lose me."

Mary has no problems recalling how restrictive her upbringing was. "There were things that I wanted to do that other people did, that I wasn't allowed to do because my parents were always so fearful. Once, when I was an early teen, all of my friends went on a hayride and my father and mother were afraid to let me go because they had heard that sometimes there's a fire on a hayride, that sometimes the kids smoke. So I couldn't go." Mary's response would be to "get hysterical. I would be so upset and so angry. But I can see now the way my parent treated me instilled a great deal of fear in me, because what's modeled for you is what you absorb. I didn't realize until my divorce how fearful a person I was. I always thought I was a very strong person. And then I realized all those things out there that I was no longer protected from. You know, I'm just learning how to come out of the fear and have some faith in God, which I do, and some faith in myself, which I do. But I didn't have any of those things before and didn't understand that they were even necessary, because I was always taken care of."

Mary's mother was a housewife. Even though Mary was born toward the end of the Depression, her mother didn't work because "it was more important, as far as my parents were concerned, for me to be taken care of." For a while her parents had tough times financially. "Later on my dad—he was a salesman in men's clothing—did better. By that time I was pretty well grown, but still they never deprived me of anything. They would deprive themselves rather than deprive me. I had dancing lessons and I had, in high school, cashmere sweaters, when my parents went without. And, of course, I didn't understand that or realize that and they probably did me a disservice by that, because it was overindulgence."

Her parents continued to overprotect her even as an adult, which disturbed her as much as it had when she was a child. Mary was especially frustrated by the daily attention and visits she received from her parents when her first child was born. "I realized soon that I was in big trouble, because they lived in the same neighborhood and they began to drop over just about every day. I had very little privacy and I didn't want to hurt their feelings. One thing I did have for them—even if it wasn't a lot of respect—was definitely a love and a fear of hurting their feelings, a fear of abusing them, because one of the things they let me know was how much they loved me. And that can be a real guilt trip."

Mary was burdened with guilt because "the thing my father and mother kept saying to me was, 'We would give up our lives for you.' I didn't realize how much of a guilt trip that was until I was older. In fact, only recently when I went into therapy did I realize what a terrible burden that is to lay on a child because you're saying, 'I would do anything for you, now you have to do anything for me.' " One of the ways they exacted their repayment, Mary says, was to cause her to feel she couldn't say, "Look, I need some privacy and I don't want you coming over every day." She couldn't express those feelings, she says, "because they wouldn't understand it, because anyone who would lay down their life for me is certainly not going to understand my being so selfish as to not want them to come over every day to see their grandchild."

In addition to guilt, Mary also felt some disdain for her parents because of their self-sacrificing nature. "I was disappointed in them in some ways. Because they wanted to do so much for me they would not do enough for themselves, and I realized that when you do that, you don't have self-love and you don't have respect for yourself. If you are willing to give up everything to your child, that is wrong. Naturally you want to give your children things you didn't have, you want to give them material things so they'll be happy, but when you sacrifice yourself to do that, it's not a self-loving way. So I didn't respect them for that and I knew that it had spoiled me in very much the same way I spoiled my own children."

Mary typically demonstrated her disrespect by an obvious lack of appreciation for the "care packages" her parents frequently bestowed upon her. "My parents would come over and my mother would always bring these care packages. Instead of loving it the way I should have, I felt like I couldn't grow up and that they were trying to buy my love by doing all of these things for me. And I've done the same thing with Josh, which is why he's angry at me now." Not too long ago, Josh "cited" her for her self-sacrificing ways: "You're always giving up yourself for everybody else. You don't even appreciate yourself," he told her. And he's right, Mary says. "I've given up my whole life for everybody else so that I could be loved and wanted."

During the early years of Mary's marriage, she was motivated to work hard to get people to like her because she was very lonely, although she didn't understand what she was feeling. "My husband pretty much abandoned me. He was a workaholic. It was his style. It wasn't just to make a lot of money—it was much more. I mean, you have to understand, this man was a true workaholic. It was as much a disease as alcoholism. People would look at him and say, 'My God. What is he doing? Why does he have to work so much?' "

According to Mary, Bud's dysfunctional behavior around work was a result of his upbringing. Bud felt that he was the second-class citizen in the family, the brother who was looked down upon by his parents. "He had this incredible work ethic, which he had before I ever knew him," Mary recalls. He ran a business when he was a young kid, and before he went into the service he sold the business for quite a bit of money. This was his pattern. He avoided being with people. He avoided communication, because he had the need to succeed, which he got from his family. He was the second child. His brother was very, very much revered. Everything came harder to Bud than it did to his brother. His brother could just sort of look at the books and he'd get A's. My husband had to really struggle with the work and he'd still get C's. His brother was always athletic and succeeded in everything. Buddy was a klutz. So his way of succeeding was by succeeding in business. I only learned all that when we were in therapy for our marital problems—why his self-esteem was so low that he needed to bully me, which is what he did."

Bud had a strong and rigid personality that was very hard to live with—he always believed he was right. "He could never do anything unethical or illegal. He was a very righteous, moral person, maybe more so than he needed to be. What's right is right and he would only do what's right. And so I lived with this. My kids lived with this. He spent all of his time working, and they didn't get a lot of him. When we were together, we would be a family on the weekends, but we would more or less do what he would organize. And nobody complained. But there was a lack in my relationship with him. There was no sensuality, no sexuality—it was gone from the marriage, totally gone. And if ever I would say anything, he would make out that it was my fault: he wasn't attracted to me because I was not being sweet and kind to him. And it was very hard to be sweet and kind to him because I didn't seem to be physically attractive to him. I knew that shouldn't have been the case, because I was attractive to other men. So there was something wrong, but I never really knew it.

"I always thought it was my fault. That's what I got from parents who dealt with me the way they did. And when you think you're wrong, you become wrong. You create it in your life, which is what I ultimately did. I had a whole lot, and I lost it. Because I didn't appreciate it for what it was, because there was always something wrong and I was wrong and this wasn't right. And I never really understood what it was. A lot of it was that I was love-starved, not just sex-starved, but love-starved. Now, that had to reflect on the children. With my older kids, it reflected in that I was hard on them and I expected a lot. I didn't give them a lot of freedom, and I was very controlling."

In retrospect, Mary feels that the way she raised her older children actually produced healthier kids than the overprotecting approach to parenting she employed with Josh. "The two oldest boys grew up fine. They had their little idiosyncrasies and quirks like every kid in a family does. But they really grew up fine. One grew up to be an engineer, the other grew up to be a lawyer. Josh was born nine years after Michael and eight years after Danny. Josh was born Jesus Christ in terms of how the family responded to him. I mean, he was the second coming. He was, first of all, what the other boys weren't. He was so beautiful. Well, they were good-looking kids, they were all darling kids. But from the minute Josh was born he was big, which is always an asset for a boy. The other two were much smaller. Josh was spoiled from the minute he was born. Everybody loved the baby. The other two were old enough that they had their own lives, so they weren't jealous of him and they babied him. They loved him and Josh became obnoxious."

For the first two years of Josh's life he talked a blue streak. "We'd sit at the table having dinner and we'd say, 'We have to have current events.' Everyone would have a current event and we'd say, 'What did you get from the newspaper, Josh?' 'I read about New Nork [sic] and New Nork is a big city.' We would crack up, because he was so bright and so articulate." Josh was so spoiled that when Mary put him into nursery school, he would run into people with his bicycle because he had not been disciplined. "He was so spoiled that when people would be at the house to visit us everyone had to stop talking when Josh walked in the room."

Soon Josh was not only able to demand the attention of visitors, he was also able to claim much interest and attention from his father, something the other children had simply not been able to do. "Buddy picked Josh up when he cried, every time he cried. We had friends who would come over and say to Bud, 'Leave Josh alone. Let him cry it out.'" Bud didn't comply and Mary became envious of Josh because she felt Bud gave to Josh as a way of not giving to her. "I was jealous of my own kid, because there was no lovemaking, there was no connection like a husband and wife should have. It was all surface. We had this wonderful life. We traveled. My parents watched the kids and we would go to Mexico, and we went to Europe. We had this wonderful life and it was all lovely, except that it was all surface. And kids know when it's surface. They know when that connection is missing from parents."

Meanwhile, the two older boys became less enamored with Josh's attitude as they grew up. They began viewing Josh as "this spoiled brat, which he was," Mary says. "Josh got his way, and if he didn't get his way he would cry and he'd finally ultimately get what he wanted. So he became such a strong individual—and manipulative. He manipulated everything. He would set up competition between me and Buddy by implying that he would hate me and love Daddy if I didn't do what he wanted. And I bought into his manipulation. I really believed that Josh wouldn't love me if I really disciplined him. So he had already developed into a difficult child by the time he was two.

"I took him to a psychiatrist who worked with kids. We thought he was hyperactive because he was always screaming if he didn't get his way. As he grew older, he didn't listen in school—his mind was somewhere else. His kindergarten teacher said to me, 'Your child is an underachiever. He's very bright, but he is not paying attention, and he's not doing what he can do.' And he was already manipulating the teacher because he had learned how to manipulate us." By the time Mary was having this conversation with Josh's teacher she realized she had given in too much and had "created a monster."

How does Josh feel about himself? "He knows that he was overindulged and he hates it, but he still wants it. There's a real dichotomy. I didn't want my parents to do for me, because I wanted to feel adequate and do it myself. Yet, there was a part of me that became very lazy and wanted them to do it. There's a dynamic there that's a real push-pull in you to be grown up. I didn't like all the things that Buddy did for me, but I still did nothing as an adult. I had help in the house. I cooked, but I never cleaned, because there was always somebody to do it for me. So I never became a grown-up person, though I knew my own inadequacies. I knew I should have gone out and done more volunteer work than I did. I did some, but I didn't do enough. I should have gone out and learned something in school that would create a career for me. I actually thought about it before I became pregnant with Josh. But then we moved and we started a whole new life and there was just never time for that. But boy, I tell you now, I'm sure sorry, because the only thing I ever did was go to massage school, and that's hard work for someone my age to do. So I did it for several months, but even at that, I didn't do as well as I could have. There's a line of least resistance that people who are overindulged take. Josh went to college, but in a half-assed way. Michael and Danny really learned. Michael is a top-notch lawyer. He can write his own ticket in bankruptcy law anyplace in the whole country, because he really learned."

Beyond Josh's mediocre school performance, Mary concedes that her overprotectiveness contributed to considerably more dysfunctional behavior by the time her youngest son was 13. "He became out of control. He wasn't studying in school and he had a best friend whose brother was a real druggie and a real flake who said to Josh, 'Gee, if you want some of this pot, you can sell it to the kids at school.' This happened during a time when there was a lot of marijuana around and the authorities were already sending the narcs to the school. Josh was in junior high school, in the eighth grade, and he was 13 years old. It was right after his bar mitzvah that he bought some of this stuff from his friend's brother and took it to school in a Dungeons and Dragons box, because what did he know from taking a little bit and selling it undercover? He made a whole big thing of it—he was a big show-off and he got caught. I came to pick him up from school one day and was told, 'Your son is in jail.' I said, 'For what?' I was hysterical. And they said that he was caught selling marijuana and they were suspending him and throwing him out of school."

Josh was sent to another junior high school, where he made new friends and seemed to be doing all right. Yet his demeanor at home was another story. "He was a very angry kid. He didn't do what he was supposed to do at home. He didn't take the trash out when he was supposed to and he resented things. And then one day he went out with a friend with whom he was going to stay overnight. This was a nice Israeli boy. I thought everything was fine. He seemed like a lovely boy and he drove. This was when Josh was about 15, the friend was 16. They stayed at this boy's house and it just so happened that his mother had received in the mail, by mistake, a neighbor's department store credit card. She accidentally opened it and then said to her son, 'Would you please go and return this to the neighbor?' The boy took the card and he and Josh went to the store. They bought something—I don't remember what it was. The store clerks at some point realized that these kids had a stolen credit card and called the police, and the boys were arrested."

Josh ended up with a probation officer, who told Mary and Bud, "You have a couple of choices. He can either go to juvenile hall, which is a nasty place, or you can find a school for him." Mary says, "We thought we would have to send him away, and what we had in mind was something like an Outward Bound kind of program. We couldn't find anything. Josh had been in therapy prior to that, from the time he was thrown out of the other school, and it really wasn't doing any good. He didn't like the therapist, he didn't confide in him. It was not the therapist, it was Josh's way at the time—he was very belligerent and angry. Finally, this therapist called us one day and said that he had a patient who had found a school for her son that sounded like just what I was looking for. Prior to this, we had gone to many school placement counselors trying to find an appropriate school for Josh and had just about come to the conclusion that what we wanted didn't exist. Many schools would not take problem children, which is what Josh was considered."

Though at first Josh didn't like the therapeutic boarding school to which he was sent—the Spring Creek Community located in Montana—he remained there for two years and did very well. "He really learned a lot. He learned to love philosophy. He had a wonderful education. The educator there was a most inspiring schoolteacher. His subject was philosophy. And Josh always said he wanted to be a philosophy teacher. And, believe me, if he weren't so materialistic and didn't want the finer things in life that he grew up with, he would do that, because it's still his favorite subject. For the most part, he turned out much better because of the Spring Creek experience."

Two years later, though, when he left Spring Creek Community, Mary and Bud did not allow Josh to return to their home. "We knew we couldn't bring him back home because it would start all over again. We didn't feel equipped, yet, to handle him. So we put him into a private residential school called the Happy Valley School in Ojai, California, that has as its mission to teach its pupils to learn how to live with people of all nations rather than to place an emphasis on academics. They have in their charter a requirement that a third of their population must be foreign students from all over the world."

Despite the humanitarian aspects of the school, it was a very difficult transition for Josh, Mary remembers. "It was difficult for Josh to move from a cloistered environment like Spring Creek into the real world. At Spring Creek, anytime he felt sad, he had a counselor to tell his troubles to. And even though Happy Valley wasn't a highly academic school, because Josh has this real perfectionistic quality, as I do and as he learned from his father, anything short of straight A's was unacceptable to Josh. Josh felt he had to really perform. He worked so hard and it was so hard for him, because it was a different type curriculum. So he developed high blood pressure." Josh eventually calmed down, graduated from Happy Valley, and went on to attend Pitzer University, one of the Claremont Colleges in Claremont, California.

Mary and Bud, however, had not fared as well as Josh over this same period of time, even though they had attended group parenting sessions when Josh was at Spring Creek. Mary ascribes their stunted development to the fact that she and her husband remained in denial throughout the process. "What we did is we lied. We had no relationship, no intimate relationship. Everything was surface, but we really didn't know how to make it another way. Buddy is very rigid and things have to be just this certain way and perfect. And his way of having a good time is really dissecting it, not just having a good time. It's hard to explain, but I never understood those things, and so we didn't have any kind of a real intimate connection. We pretended that everything was wonderful, you know. And so we got to believe our own story."

However, just before Josh graduated from Happy Valley, Mary made up her mind to leave her husband. She decided to tell Josh—a decision she now regrets. "I actually went there to Happy Valley and told Josh. I probably destroyed him. I mean, the things I think of that I've done. If it would help to cut off my right arm, I would do it. But it wouldn't help, and I've got to stop punishing myself for it."

Josh was stunned. Mary's parents and Bud's parents were also "beside themselves." But, she says, "I couldn't live the lie any longer. I just couldn't. So I blew a whole wonderful life as it looked like then. I mean, I've given up a lot. It's been a very tough road these three years for me. But there's been so much growth."

One of the more significant lessons Mary has learned has to do with her overprotecting way of raising children. "I've learned that it's so important to let them make their own decisions once they are old enough to do that. It's so important that they feel good about the decisions that they make or they understand the consequences of the poor ones. If they are allowed that, then even if they make a mistake, next time they'll choose better. You can't keep rescuing them."

Right now, Mary's relationship with her youngest son is improving, though there are still flare-ups. Josh so identifies with his mother that he is living vicariously through her experiences and attempts to grow, and she has yet to live up to his high expectations. "He is wanting me to become an adult. He wants to see me successful, because he relates so much to me that he knows that if I'm successful in my life and if I'm a happy

person, which I'm learning to be, that he will be able to attain some measure of happiness also." She admits, then, that "Josh is in a place of not yet
accepting responsibility for himself. He still feels like a victim."

The recent arguments between Mary and Josh center around these
very issues. Josh is angry because he feels victimized by Mary's decision
to end her marriage and by her recovery process, which is providing her
with the strength to abandon her overprotective model of parenting. Josh
feels Mary has lied to him all of his life. Mary, on the other hand, feels a bit
victimized herself by Josh's anger and willingness to lash out at her. "I said
to him after this last fight that we had, 'Josh, you're a victim. Until you start
to take responsibility for yourself, you're going to be a victim.' And he said,
'You're right. I am. You're right. But I'm not ready to do anything about it
yet.' And I said, 'Your choice,' and he left very angrily." Though Mary took a
tough stance, she still felt some guilt. "The point is he feels abused and
abandoned. He has no home any longer. It was devastating to him that
Bud and I had to sell that house. It was the only house he ever knew. And I
don't have a room for him here, which I should have." After a pause, she
regroups and goes on to say, "In reality it's better that it's this way, because
it's going to be hard now, but he will learn that he must be responsible for
himself."

She had even promised herself that this time she would not be the
one to call Josh first to make up. "Well, I called him yesterday and I
thought, 'He's going to really be pissed and he's not going to talk.' Instead,
he was so happy. He didn't say it, but he was. And I was almost in tears,
because I didn't know what his response would be. All I know is that I
love that kid so much I can't even begin to tell you. It would be very easy
for me to give in and let Josh step on me my whole life, because that's how
much I love him. But I have to love myself enough to get what I need, and
what I need is not to be stepped on. Josh is going to be all right, because
I'm going to be all right and because I will not take any more abuse from
him. And I'm getting therapy to help me do that."

Michael

Michael, 30, works hard and plays hard—and is very protective of his
free time. He would not allow this interview to take place during the
weekend, for example, because, he says with conviction, "That's my
time." A bankruptcy attorney during the week, Michael spends Saturdays
and Sundays participating in rodeos throughout the nation. "I've always
ridden horses and I've always owned horses, but I now have a huge ranch
with cattle and horses and I now rodeo all over the state and out of the

state. It's a lot of fun and it's really something that I've always wanted to do and just never said to myself, 'Hey, go do it. Spend the money on yourself and have a good time.' For so long I denied myself this hobby—I denied it economically and I denied it timewise. Now I'm doing what really turns me on."

Michael did not always run his life in a way that provided self-satisfaction. Instead, he admits that during his first and only marriage he was self-sacrificing. In fact, one of the most important things that he learned from that marriage is "you don't put yourself second. Put yourself equal. I didn't do that. If we both wanted something and we obviously could only afford one item, for instance, I would buy for her what she wanted because I felt she should have it rather than me. So that would be a self-sacrifice. And I did that many times." In terms of his personal life, then, Michael notes that he has been a lot like his mother.

In most other ways, however, he identifies very closely with his father with the same intensity that Mary identifies with Josh. "I probably relate to my dad better than to my mom, because we are very much alike in a lot of respects—mannerisms, method of thinking, method of acting." He adds, "Neither Josh nor Danny related to my father as well as I did, because their personalities were very similar to my mother's."

Michael describes his father as being a very dedicated person. "When he starts something he will definitely finish it. He's conscientious. He takes pride in his work, so he won't do anything half-assed. And he's pretty intense." He views his mother, on the other hand, as "more sensitive, less structured, less rigorous." Michael views his brother Josh as a lot more easygoing than he. "He's less concerned about tomorrow and more concerned about today and the immediate future and immediate pleasure. I think I act and react as a result of taking into consideration more issues than Josh does."

Michael, who is nine years older than Josh, was not around when his younger brother started to get into trouble, but he was not surprised when he began to hear the news from his mother. "I knew that he was out of hand. Josh really was a rebellious kid and I guess I attributed the problems he was having to being rebellious." Michael believes he understands why Josh became the problem kid: "He had very little discipline in his life, whether that was on his own or discipline by my folks. As a result I think he sort of did what he wanted, when he wanted, at anybody else's expense. And he had very little direction."

Michael feels that he did not behave as his younger brother behaved because he attempted to pattern himself after his father. "I followed in business as he did. And I think that created the discipline for me. If you want to do something, you have to take what steps are necessary to get to that point. And since I chose to follow in the business that my dad did, I created my own discipline."

The downside of Michael's identification with his father is his workaholic bent. "I was a workaholic like my father was a workaholic. But both he and I have changed considerably. I used to come in to work at seven A.M. and stay until eight or nine every night. Now I get in at seven or seven-thirty A.M., but I stay until about five-thirty or six. So I'm working fewer hours. I'm taking it a little bit less seriously. I am also able at work to say, 'No, I don't have the time to do that.' I think my dad has recognized that he needs time to do things for himself and have fun other than just being out there trying to earn a living."

Like his father, Michael was propelled into changing his life when his marriage fell apart. "There were some great lessons. There was a lack of communication, a lack of working at a relationship. I've now realized that that's something that you have to continue to do as time goes on. Just because you have a piece of paper that says you're married doesn't mean that you don't have to work at that relationship any further." He adds, "I wasn't taught by my father to communicate. So maybe that's something I would have had my dad do differently, although I still don't think I would say, 'Hey, you should have taught me to communicate better.' "

Postscript

This family's dysfunctional dynamic has varied from child to child. On the face of it, the two elder sons were raised under a more demanding parent mode, while the youngest, Josh, was pampered to excess. Mary and Bud responded to Josh's every whim in order to compete for his love and control his life. Josh soon took on the classic characteristics of the overprotected child who becomes the ultimate prima donna. He learned to manipulate his parents and then expanded his experiment to test others in his environment, including his teachers. Josh, however, wasn't the only child in this family affected by his exposure to overprotective parents. Michael was impacted in a different though just as dysfunctional manner by his parents' overprotective style—he treated his former wife in much the same way that his mother had handled Josh. To that end, Michael behaved as if he was a second-class citizen when dealing with his wife. He routinely acquiesced to his wife's wishes, particularly when it came to making purchases. Typically, he subordinated his own needs to meet her desires.

From talking with this family and from my experience with my current husband, the most significant lesson I have learned about overprotective parents is the underlying role that fear plays in propelling the co-dependent behavior of such parents and their children. Basically, mothers and fathers who smother their children are parents who are afraid of losing the love of their offspring or losing their offspring altogether. My husband's mother feared that if she wasn't overindulgent she would somehow be rejected by her son as she had been rejected by her husband. Mary's parents never forgot how close they had come to losing at birth the only child they would ever have. Mary herself was an overprotective mother because she genuinely believed she was in competition with her husband for Josh's love. And Michael believed, on some level, that the way to his former wife's heart was through the voluntary subordination of his needs and desires to hers.

To determine what role, if any, fear plays in the way you are raising your children, make a list of at least five activities that you really did not want to do but that you performed for the benefit of your child. For example, did you spend a lot of money for a motorcycle that causes you great concern every time your child starts it up? Do you buy your children expensive clothes they don't need and rarely wear? Once you have made your list, write down in as much detail as possible under each item what motivated you to do something that went against your better judgment.

CHAPTER 6

THE DISENGAGING PARENT

As a child I felt unloved, so I struggled mightily to deny feelings of inadequacy. My youthful attempts to suppress such painful emotions caused me to behave erratically: I either lashed out angrily at others, or succumbed comfortably to my mother's punishments, which required me to be housebound and thus socially isolated for months at a time. In later years, I turned my aggression toward the achievement of professional goals and became a bionic woman of sorts, masking my low self-esteem behind a work ethic that was not only socially isolating but emotionally restrictive as well. I was generally too busy or too tired to undertake the day-to-day tasks and endearments associated with healthy parenting. Indeed, I used my workaholism as an excuse to dodge, as much as possible, responsibility for raising my son. My story, then, is a tale of how a disengaging adolescent, adult, and, finally, parent is created.

I have been governed, for as long as I can remember, by an underlying insecurity about my overall self-worth. This pervasive insecurity was an all-important factor that influenced my disengaging behavior. My inferiority complex was largely provoked by a heartfelt belief that no matter what I accomplished, it would not be enough to win my mother's love. When I made good grades, for instance, my mother gave me very little acknowledgment. She said only, "You're smart, you're supposed to do well." So I grew up believing that only truly exceptional behavior would stir my mother to demonstrate pride in my achievements. And since I rarely received such a response from her, I assumed my accomplishments simply were not worth noting—though I never gave up trying to gain her approval, which, for me, was synonymous with gaining her love.

I was also wary of my father's love because I questioned his integrity and loyalty. Though he often would pull me aside to offer strategies for how to best "get back" at my mother, he would just as often refuse to take a public stand on my behalf and thus directly oppose my mother's demanding behavior. From my point of view, then, my father's stealthy behavior seemed like cowardice born from a lack of genuine affection for me. In other words, if he really loved me he would stand tall and protect me. Since such a scenario rarely played itself out, there were times when I wondered if he loved me at all. In addition, I lived with a nagging though never articulated suspicion that if in fact my father didn't love me, perhaps it was because I didn't deserve his love.

So I entered adulthood striving to prove to my parents my value in the hope that I would eventually win their love. Ironically, the workaholic strategy I used to try to gain acclaim and recognition from my parents led to my becoming a disengaging parent who was rarely available to provide my own son the love and nurturing he needed. Further, my strategy didn't end up changing my perceptions of how my parents felt about me. Obtaining a college degree had several beneficial outcomes that were obvious and some not so obvious. Certainly there are economic gains to be made from a college education. However, I chiefly was motivated to graduate from college because I thought such an achievement would win my parents' love once and for all. I even tried to set up an insurance policy for myself to ensure that I achieved the ultimate goal of parental approval. My first semester, for example, I worked hard to attain a straight-A average. Then I started to worry that making straight A's might not be enough to secure my parents' love, so I determined that I would obtain a bachelor's degree in three years instead of the normal four, with a record of straight A's. But after a semester or two I came to the conclusion that that might not do it, so I cut the time down to two and one-half years and majored in economics with a minor in math. Still uncertain as to whether such achievements would impress my mother into giving me the accolades I craved, I sought and won a summer school scholarship from Harvard University to study economic development and philosophy. When I graduated summa cum laude and my parents and siblings drove from their home in Los Angeles to the New York campus to witness the event, and then visited for less than 24 hours before traveling to Philadelphia to spend days with their friends, I was crushed and angry. From my point of view, all of my work was for naught. My relationship with my parents remained the same and I still felt unloved. Meanwhile, I had virtually abandoned my four-year-old son as I pursued my obsession.

Tracking the evolution of how I became a disengaging, overachieving adult and parent has led me to yet another ironic conclusion: My obsessive attempts to be the best and the brightest were modeled after my mother. Indeed, my mother's high expectations for me were the mirror image of those she maintained for herself. Mother was an ambitious woman who spent much of her time either teaching or attending graduate school to move up the career ladder. She succeeded, and eventually became a high school principal. I also succeeded in terms of my career accomplishments. But neither one of us did as well with our children as we would have liked, since we didn't know how to nurture, how to love.

"YOU SIMPLY ARE NOT THAT IMPORTANT TO ME"

Classically disengaging mothers and fathers are either too busy, too tired, or too sick to personally parent their children. Mostly they are afraid of the emotional commitment and responsibility entailed in raising a child and maintaining a marriage or involvement in any type of relationship that requires nurturing. Indeed, a causal factor that is shared by all manner of disengaging parents is that loving is difficult for them because their own upbringing was loveless or inadequate in that regard. So they hide behind their ambition, or they manage to stay exhausted from either work or play, or they use illness—real and imaginary—to keep a safe distance from the emotional demands of their children. The message, then, that they give to their sons and daughters is, "You simply are not that important to me."

Children of unavailable or preoccupied parents are prone to refer to themselves in a demeaning manner, such as, "What I think isn't that important," or "I don't really like myself." These children feel abandoned and rejected by their parents, although, for a number of reasons, they tend to deny what they see and the emotional pain they feel. Such children often close their eyes to their abandonment because it's too painful to confront, especially since what is being implicitly conveyed is that the child is not important enough to spend time with and thus to love. In addition, such young people often are confused as to what they should feel. If the parent's workaholism has led to a high-paying job, for instance, the child is conflicted as to the appropriateness of feeling abandoned. After all, doesn't the child reap the benefits of the parent's career success? So feelings of anger and frustration give way to feelings of guilt. When, at 19, I decided to attend college after having married, had a child, and left my husband, I knew it meant that I would have precious little time to spend with my son. I pursued my goal primarily because of my own insecurities about needing to prove myself worthy of my parents' love, but I told my son only about what my college degree would do for his financial future.

I used guilt to mitigate his anger and frustration about my shifting him from one babysitter to another (during one semester he spent time with three different babysitters each day) in order for me to complete college in a short time with a high grade-point average. In the morning, he was awakened early enough to be dropped off at the babysitter in time for me to make an 8:00 A.M. class. By noon, I rushed back to pick him up in order to change his clothes and escort him to his kindergarten class. Then I drove back to the university to attend my afternoon classes. I could not get back in time to pick my son up from kindergarten, so I arranged to have the mother of one of his classmates pick him up and take him to her home for an hour and one-half until I could leave the campus. We went home, where I prepared dinner, and then took him to a third babysitter so that I could attend evening classes.

My five-year-old's response to his frenetic schedule was classic for children of disengaging parents. He felt anger mixed with both pride and shame—anger about being shuttled about so hurriedly and insensitively; pride about my scholastic achievements; and shame about my general lack of interest in his life as compared to the parents of his friends. My son's response was classic also in that he did not express his anger to me directly. Instead, he began to act out in his kindergarten class, particularly when he was instructed to prepare for dismissal. I was called in for a parent-teacher conference and told that my son would throw an uncontrollable tantrum if he was asked to move quickly to get ready to leave class. The teacher, it turns out, represented yet another adult who rushed him from one destination to another, and he resented his instructor's actions as he resented my behavior. Even at five years old my son understood that spending quality time with him was not one of my top priorities.

Children of mothers or fathers who are hypochondriacs—another type of disengaging parent—are also emotionally conflicted about their abandonment. They are generally plagued with both anger and guilt, as are the children of parents who work hard at unglamorous jobs that leave them too exhausted to perform more than the most cursory of parental responsibilities.

BECOMING AWARE

Recently I was reminded of a statement I once made to justify my workaholism and willingness to allow my son (and at times my marriages) to come second to my professional life: "I focus as much as I do on my career because there's a direct relationship between effort expended and the return on that effort. With children and husbands there are no guarantees." Now I wince when I hear what I once touted. Fortunately, I never repeated this philosophy to my son. I did, however, express such sentiments to my second husband. Needless to say, we divorced not long after my declaration.

The following is a list of comments that are typical of disengaging parents such as myself. The statements are not as direct as my aforementioned rationalization, but the message conveyed is pretty much the same: Loved ones are not that important. It is important, though, that you become aware of how it is possible to demoralize your child by what your language implies. Again, quotes collected by teachers from the Hacienda —La Puente School District are provided for insight and revelation.

- "I'm too busy. Maybe later."
- "I can't promise you."
- "Can't you see I'm busy?"
- "Maybe tomorrow."
- "I might get to it tomorrow."
- "I never wanted a child in the first place."
- "You were an accident."

Disengaging parents, then, undermine their children's self-esteem by ignoring their emotional needs. Basically such parents do not listen to their children because they are afraid the children may need more from them than they are emotionally equipped to give. But unlike demanding and critical parents, who don't listen because they believe so strongly in their own point of view, disengaging parents feign an interest in their children's emotional concerns and then procrastinate to avoid ever having to make good on their promises. Many of these parents are just as angry as their children, because they are equally unhappy about how they were raised, although such parents are likely to suppress or deny their feelings.

Wendy, the mother in this chapter's family profile, is a case in point. She was raised by a father who was a community leader in the Washington, D.C., neighborhood where she was born and raised. Wendy remembers how her family often attended dinners that honored the special volunteer work her father undertook to help children in need. She also recalls how her father, a police officer by profession, wasn't home that much and how she wondered sometimes if he wasn't a better father to the children in the street than he was to his own family. There is a tightness in her voice when she makes this statement.

On the face of it, Wendy is open and ready to talk about her childhood experiences and what has happened since she went out on her own, dropped out of college, married, had a child, and divorced after about four years of living through something that was less than wedded bliss. She is difficult to pin down, however, because she tends to stop just short of admitting that she feels pain. One senses a stoicism that borders on martyrdom when talking to Wendy, especially as she recounts the events that led to her having to put her only child, Karma, 19, out of her house on February 22, 1987—a date that is apparently etched in Wendy's mind.

The daughter's final departure from her mother's home also left its mark on Karma's psyche, but she sees the event as having been a liberating experience rather than traumatic. In fact, Karma for the most part exhibits a great deal of emotional detachment when talking about her mother. The tone of her discussion is often very casual, matter-of-fact, no matter how explosive the topic. During the interview, she offers a clue as to why she reacts this way: "I never really bonded with my mother as a mother. My grandmother raised me until I was 12. So my grandmother was my mother. That's who I bonded with. I've always looked at my mother in a sisterly way."

Wendy is a retired police officer who admits that she was every bit as much of a workaholic as her father, and she believes that such habits contributed to the deterioration of her relationship with her daughter. For the last few years she has been in therapy, trying to sort out how to handle her life given a shocking medical diagnosis: Wendy has multiple sclerosis. The introspection is beginning to pay off in that she is learning how to listen to her daughter and respond to Karma's emotional needs. To that end, she was pleased when her daughter invited her on a recent Sunday outing to view a sculpture called *The Awakening*. It was the first friendly overture Karma had made toward her mother in about two years. A happy Wendy reports that the day went well and the artwork's title was symbolically apropos, since it reflected what took place that day between mother and daughter.

FAMILY PROFILE:

Wendy and Karma

"I'm 40 going on 100 years old" is the way Wendy describes herself. She laughs when she makes this statement, but only slightly. A few years ago Wendy discovered that she has multiple sclerosis, a chronic and progressive ailment that typically leads to partial or complete paralysis and jerking muscles. Right now she's at a stable stage of the disease, but the list of infirmities brought on by her medication and the illness itself is long, as she herself voluntarily describes in some detail. Her recitation is bittersweet, characterized by a strained bravado that is hard to believe. "I'm now considered legally blind. My kidney function has been damaged, and I've lost some teeth. I'm losing muscle mass, have a spasmodic bladder and have had to catheterize myself. I'm losing feeling in my legs and abdomen, having problems with my colon, and can no longer walk unassisted. I use arm crutches for short distances and a wheelchair for visits to the local shopping malls." She pauses a moment, as if waiting for my reaction, then chuckles abruptly and continues to tell me about her life.

Wendy, who never remarried after her breakup approximately 16 years ago, lives alone. When asked if it is really in her best interest to live in such a solitary fashion, Wendy answers that she wants to hold on to her independence for as long as possible and expects nothing from her family members, including Karma, her 19-year-old daughter. Wendy believes she is following in her mother's footsteps in terms of how she feels her life should be run. "My mother used humor as a way of coping. Her life expectancy wasn't long, but you would never have known it." Also, like her own mother, Wendy says that she doesn't like anyone knowing how much pain she really feels—particularly emotional pain.

Karma, however, views Wendy through a more critical and, perhaps, a more revealing eye. She believes Wendy has tried to control her by using the sickness to become a heroic martyr. And, to that end, Karma has taken a hard-line stance: "When my mother first got sick, she refused my help because she wanted to be independent. So after a while I stopped offering. Then my mother wanted and needed help, but wouldn't ask for it—she expected me to use my keen intuition to determine what she needed. I won't offer anymore. If she needs help, she has a mouth and she's going to have to use her mouth to ask for help."

Wendy lives in a four-bedroom house in Washington, D.C. She receives a retirement income from her 12 years on the local police force and has a little inheritance remaining from her father's death in 1986. Karma is a full-time researcher for a government agency in the District of Columbia and has a part-time job as a political pollster. She lives in a small rented house. Wendy states that she in part subsidizes Karma's rent.

Wendy

"My mother was everything, the disciplinarian and the nurturer, because Father was seldom home," says Wendy, the third child of four and the only daughter. Still, Wendy considers her upbringing to have been good, and particularly delights in describing her mother's personality. "My mother cursed quite artfully. She was very blunt and would pretty much cut to the chase at the drop of a hat. She also was an avid reader and sometimes would read 12 books at a time." When Wendy was about 13 years old, however, her mother was diagnosed as having rheumatoid arthritis and lupus, a disease characterized by skin lesions. Wendy recalls that her mother began to do "wacky things at first, because of the high dosage of medication she had to take." For instance, as her mother lost weight because of her illness, she purchased support hose that she stuffed with sanitary pads to make her legs look bigger.

Wendy's father was a police officer who was very involved in community affairs, particularly with groups such as the Boys' Club. Wendy remembers her dad being honored at dinners because of his volunteer work with young people. Though she recalls attending some of these functions with her father, it was usually her brothers who were recruited by her dad to participate in the fun activities. "I was discouraged from being a tomboy. I think my father would have preferred a more dainty girl, but that wasn't me." Even though her father did not want her to follow in his footsteps, Wendy eventually became a police officer. Assigned to the child abuse division of the police department, she devoted her life to helping troubled children. Her father's legacy also included a history of workaholism and some resentment on the part of his daughter. "I often felt he was everybody else's father except ours."

Ironically, years later Wendy found that she was devoting 12- and 13-hour shifts to working with abused children in lieu of spending time with her own daughter. An angry Karma responded to her apparent abandonment by locking her mother out of the house. Wendy believes Karma did it intentionally. "I would get home in the middle of the night sometimes and Karma would have put the chain lock on the door so that I couldn't get in. I would have to go to my squad car and radio back to the [police] station that I needed someone to call my house to tell Karma to come open the door. It happened so often, my radio calls became a joke at the precinct." When asked why she worked so much overtime that it was virtually impossible for her to spend quality time with her daughter, Wendy replied, "I couldn't leave those other kids hanging."

Wendy married at 19 while she was attending college with a major in art. Her parents didn't want her to marry, but to finish college. She did not complete her studies, opting to have a child and be a "good wife" instead. It wasn't long, though, before she came to the realization that "there was more to being a wife than just being a wife," she says with a chuckle. First, she learned that her husband's "word did not mean what I thought it should mean." She explains: "A check bounced because the teller made a mistake, not because there wasn't any money in the bank. That works once, but not forever." The marriage came to an end after only four years. "One day I came home and my husband's secretary was in the kitchen cooking."

Wendy left her husband shortly after she witnessed that incident. She found that the police department provided her with the best income opportunity to raise her daughter in a middle-class manner, especially since her former husband did not pay child support. Karma attended private schools and was sent on trips to Africa, Spain, and Brazil. Meanwhile, Wendy spent even more time away from home, sometimes working two jobs, to provide Wendy every possible advantage. At Christmastime, for example, Wendy would work at a second job, preferably at a women's clothing store so that she could get discounts on Karma's outfits. "Karma was healthy and a good child in the beginning, even though the first two years I was in uniform I had a terrible schedule and she had to spend a lot of time with my mother."

When Karma was about 12 or 13, her behavior changed. "She started sneaking out while I was at work. But we still got along, so I wasn't too worried." Then Wendy's mother died. "I spent so much time taking care of the rest of the family and dealing with their loss, I didn't spend enough time helping my daughter. And Karma is very much like me—she contains her feelings. So she expressed to me that everything was okay with her, and I didn't really take the time to check it out." A couple of years later, the relationship between mother and daughter went into a tailspin when Wendy's illness was diagnosed. "I discovered I was sick in early 1983. I was losing weight and fatigued easily and had a dragging right foot. These were the first signs. I went to the police department's doctor and was told that I was just depressed and burned out from my schedule and the demands of my work. Finally, on a really, really hot day I had to go to the police firing range to requalify myself [a yearly requirement for police officers] and was surprised to learn that my trigger finger was getting tired quickly. Also, I could barely make it up a hill, my right foot was dragging so." She was eventually referred to a neurologist, who made the dreaded diagnosis of multiple sclerosis. Wendy continued to work for the police department on less demanding assignments until she became too weak to perform even those duties. In 1986, she retired after 12 years on the police force.

Karma's reaction to Wendy's illness was to pull away. "I think Karma tried to disassociate herself from me, because it would be easier not to like me than to face losing me. She saw a lot of things that were scary.

There were times when I could not lift my body weight, so I would fall and have to spend many hours on the floor. I had a portable potty on the floor next to the bed, and Karma wouldn't dump it for me. And when she came in from school, she wouldn't say 'Hi.' She wouldn't ask me if I wanted a glass of water, and she knew I had been confined to bed all day. But she would come in and go to the farthest room in the house."

To make matters worse, "Karma was no longer acting in the role of the child as I wanted her to. Instead, she behaved like the adult, like the parent. The balance between friend and parent is very tenuous. For a long time, Karma and I were more like friends. But when it came time to be a parent, our friendship came to an end." During this period, Karma also began to "roll her eyes" a lot and talk back to Wendy, which provoked Wendy into doing what she swore she would never do. "My mother would slap me, which is one of the most demeaning measures of discipline. And I knew better because I taught effective parenting skills to the women I came in contact with as a police officer in the child abuse unit. Still, I ended up doing to Karma what my mother did to me."

The problems were exacerbated by Karma's discovery of what had heretofore been a well-kept secret of her mother's life. "My longtime boyfriend was a good influence on Karma until Karma found out he was married. She was about 14 or 15 years old when she found out, and that's when I think she really lost respect for me." Wendy eventually gave up the boyfriend as a lover but he continues to come around from time to time as a platonic friend. "About three or four years ago when I was really sick, I could see on his face that he was worried and that he was being pulled in many directions. So I told him I couldn't have sex anymore. I lied to let him off the hook. The way I figured it, if he up and left his wife when I was sick, I would feel he had done it because I was sick, which isn't the right reason, since he wouldn't leave his wife when I wasn't ill."

Meanwhile, Karma and Wendy were experiencing what Wendy refers to as "the thunderstorm and the rainbow—we were having a lot of storms and no rainbows." The acrimony between mother and daughter reached such a level that Wendy declared, "This four-bedroom, two-bath house isn't big enough for the two of us." She set a date in March of 1987 for Karma's departure to go live with her father, who had remarried. On February 22, 1987, however, Wendy asked Karma where she had been and was told, "None of your business." Wendy's response: "We need not wait until March, you need to go now." Karma left, but soon found out that she felt pretty uncomfortable with her father and stepmother. Wendy, however, did not let her return.

A few months later, Karma, who had won a number of college scholarships, graduated from high school and opted not to go to any of the universities that had accepted her. "It really blew my mind. I thought everything was good, and then I discovered that everything that I wanted for Karma she didn't want for herself. She told me that she had never wanted to go on her trips to Africa, Spain, and Brazil. She said she went because I wanted her to go. I was really shaken. Everything that I had thought I was supposed to do had meant nothing." Wendy believes, however, that had she not been ill, things might have turned out differently. "I was sick. I didn't have the strength in me that I normally have. Otherwise I would have driven her to the university's door and delivered her to the classroom if that's what it took to get her to go. But I just didn't have the fight. And that's one thing that I regret."

During this rebellion Karma accused Wendy of trying to be the martyr, the hero, and of using her illness to try to control Karma. Wendy disagreed. "I wasn't trying to be a martyr or a hero. I am very, very conscious of independence. I am not a good care receiver. I am very independent. I resent having to ask for help. I like to be a caregiver. That's how I get my rewards, my good strokes." To that end, even though Wendy has three professionally successful brothers, she was the primary caretaker for her father when he was sick, up until his death five years after her mother's. Wendy herself was sick during this period.

Wendy also is involved in a telephone reassurance program that involves her maintaining contact with 13 elderly ladies. "I call at least two or three of the ladies a day, just to let them know that somebody cares about them."

These days, Wendy and Karma are talking more on the phone and spending a little more time with each other, because they, too, are beginning to learn how to let each other know that they care. "I'm not an active church person, but I do talk to God and I do see a psychiatrist. So it feels good that after two years of Karma not making any offers for us to spend time together, she invited me out for a Sunday afternoon."

Wendy has had a lot of time to reflect on the role she has played [or not played] in her daughter's life now that she spends much of her life bedridden—and she has some regrets and some pride about the way things turned out. "I think that I didn't allow enough time to be with Karma when she was growing up. And because I was busy, I don't think that I followed through on punishments like I should have. I might put Karma on a two-week punishment and then forget and only enforce a one-week punishment. But sometimes I look at Karma and I'm very, very proud, because she's the type of person who will make it. She has to make it. She has to prove that she can do it." Wendy is gleeful about a recent conversation she had with her daughter in which Karma informed her that she now wants to go college. Though Karma has debts and responsibilities from having purchased an expensive car, Wendy is convinced that she will somehow pull it off. "Her head is turning in the right direction—finally."

As for what direction Wendy's head is turning in terms of her own future, the picture is more oblique. She says, for example, that at one point her psychiatrist diagnosed her as being "organically depressed." Wendy also mentions that she has a philosophy about death and suicide. "I believe that a person has choices, and that suicide is a legitimate choice, if it's done in a way that is not detrimental to others." Her attitude about herself and the way she would like others to see her is summed up, perhaps, by a line from a poem that she read to me, which was written by a woman who had lived in a nursing home for the elderly: "When you look at me, look a little deeper."

Karma

Upbeat and with a droll sense of humor, Karma often uses a quip to take the sting out of serious topics. She's pretty and has a girlish-sounding voice that belies a fiercely independent and feisty character. Karma is very opinionated about her past, particularly the role her mother played in her life. She feels she had a "good upbringing, but it was my grandmother who raised me, because my mother was a workaholic." Wendy's work patterns proved to be an ongoing source of contention. "When we got into battles over her workaholism, my mother always told me, 'I'm doing it for you.' And I kept saying, 'Don't do that.' " Karma lived with her grandmother until she was about 12, when Wendy decided her daughter was old enough to stay home by herself. Karma's life changed once she returned to live with her mother.

"I had a happy childhood living with my grandmother. She exposed me to a lot of things. We would go to the ballet, things like that. My grandmother got me started on my favorite hobby—shopping—which conflicted a lot with what my mother was trying to do. My grandmother had me living an extravagant life, and I guess my mother thought she couldn't live up to the expectations as far as the things she could buy in comparison to what my grandmother would get me. So I acquired my grandmother's tastes, while my mother still had her tastes, and that caused a conflict."

At first, Karma did not feel conflict about leaving her grandmother to move back with her mother. "By the time I was nine, my life revolved around my bedroom anyway. And I wanted to be left alone by everybody." In addition, Wendy was working the 3:00 P.M. to 11:00 P.M. shift when Karma moved back, so "I could come home and be by myself and do whatever I wanted, as long as I cleaned up by the time my mother got home. So I had my own little life."

But relations between Karma and her mother soon became strained. "I will admit I was a bad 12-year-old. Every kid gets to the age when she wants to run wild and be reckless. Twelve and 13 was that age for me. I would do things like not come home on time, or sneak out of the house at night. But other than that, I never really got into too much trouble at school." But then Wendy and Karma began a "respect battle" that lasted for many years.

"She would yell at me and I would yell at her and she would tell me that I didn't respect her, because she was my mother. And I would say, 'Why should I respect you? You don't respect me as a human being. You talk to me any kind of way you want to.' So that was our main conflict. I've always felt that, regardless of your age, a person should respect you, at least as a person, and talk to you in a civil tone. So when she came at me with an uncivil tone, I came right back at her with an uncivil tone. In that way she thought I was disrespectful and I thought she was disrespectful."

Mother and daughter disagree as to who is responsible for starting these battles. "My mother says, 'It's the way it came out of my mouth.' I would say, 'It came out of my mouth because she approached me the way she did.' There were plenty of times when I would be in a pleasant mood and she would come home and just say something the wrong way and that would ruin my mood and we would be arguing five minutes later. So, we used to fight like that all of the time, but we don't fight like that anymore." Why? "I moved. That is the only thing that changed and keeps us from fighting."

Wendy's illness also has contributed to the arguments, although Karma didn't understand the significance of multiple sclerosis at first. But once she began to see her mother's physical condition deteriorate, she "felt sorry for her, because I knew she was a very strong-willed person, and that MS was taking a great toll on her. But as she got worse, she got nasty and she didn't want to face the fact that she needed help. She told everybody to leave her alone, that she could still do everything for herself, but she really couldn't, but she refused any help. I got to the point where I said, 'Well, fine. I'm not going to help you, I'm not going to do anything, because every time I try you get a nasty attitude. So, forget it.' Then when she needed it and I would not give it, she said, 'You're of no use. You're no help. You're inconsiderate. You're wrapped up in yourself. Here I am sick, and you have an attitude.' And by that time it was true. I did have an attitude, because I felt that I had tried so much before and she didn't want it. Then when she needed it, she didn't want to say that she needed it—I was just supposed to know from this keen intuition of mine what she wanted. So we battled all of the time about that."

Enmity prevailed on a number of levels between Karma and Wendy, and between Karma and Wendy's brothers concerning caretaker issues. "Although my mother was sick, she was still running to my grandfather trying to help him, and still playing mother to her brothers. After my grandmother died, my mother became everybody's mother—her father's mother, and mother to two of her brothers. She just took over the mother hen's role." When Wendy complained to her brothers that Karma wasn't helping her, Karma became extremely resentful. "I felt she was telling half a story to my relatives, because my uncle was always on my back. And I really didn't feel that my uncle could say anything to me, because the only thing he would do is come over on Sundays to eat and leave. He lived within driving distance. So he could come over and do something to help if he wanted to, and I felt that I was 15, 16, 17 years old, that I was entitled to have a life, that I was entitled to grow up, but I had to be stuck in the house taking care of her, and my uncle would have the nerve to tell me I was not a good child. So we would constantly have that fight, and I would tell him to get out of my face because he wasn't doing anything to help. I told him, 'When you start to do something, then you can get in my face.' And up until this day, he's still not doing anything to help my mother."

Wendy was apparently not playing mother to her daughter, however. Karma appears unbothered by the abandonment. "I always looked at her like a sisterly type person, anyway. I knew that she was my mother, that she had me, but I never really thought we had that motherly type bond. I did that with my grandmother; I bonded with her. So, my mother and I used to have that conflict also. Now I feel that I have a mother-daughter bonding with her, but not then."

For Karma, her freedom to do as she pleases is an important theme that she returns to over and over again during this interview. And it has been an ever-present, if not always recognized, burr in Wendy's and Karma's relationship. "When I was nine I was into my own world. I was nine when I decided that I wanted to move into my own apartment. At nine, I knew an apartment was what I needed to have. I've always felt as if I had no privacy, no matter how big the house was, no matter how big the room was. I just could not find a space that was big enough for me. Even if I had nothing to do in the space, I wanted the space. I wanted the freedom to decorate, to do what I wanted to do and not have to hear anybody's mouth, basically. So I told my mother, about a year and a half ago, that her house was not big enough for the two of our personalities to exist. By that time, she agreed."

Everything came to a head, though, shortly after Karma decided that she didn't want to go to college. "I had a hard twelfth grade and I knew I wasn't ready for college. I knew that if I went I wouldn't have done well, I would have barely made it, and then I would have had to hear the whole family's mouth. So I changed my mind and told them I wasn't going to go to college." She got a job instead, and bought her own car. With a car she had more freedom and stayed away from home as much as she could. "Just looking at the house disgusted me." It wasn't long before Karma and Wendy had a battle royal that proved to be the definitive quarrel. Wendy, returning home from a stay in the hospital, wanted to know where Karma would be if she wasn't going to be home when Wendy arrived. Karma flatly refused to tell her. "I had a doctor's appointment that day, but I felt that we didn't have the type of relationship where I felt I wanted her to know what was going on in my life. I was 18 years old and she didn't have to pay the bills for me—I was working two jobs—so I said, 'I'm not going to tell you.' So she told me that I had better tell her by the time she got home or I should be ready to leave, so I left."

Karma stayed in a motel that first night, then moved in with her father and his second wife. When that didn't work out, she got her own apartment. From Karma's point of view, now that there's been some time and space between her and her mother, their relationship has improved, although she questions Wendy's motivation. "We don't really argue anymore because she feels that I would leave and never come back. That's a silly belief, because I would come back. But I don't push her. If that's what she thinks, I don't try to correct her." These days, Karma is more attentive. She stops by fairly often to help her mother clean and she calls her regularly to see how she's doing. "We're not the best mother and daughter relationship there is on earth, but we're working at it."

Postscript

Wendy was a classic disengaging parent who was angry and who overextended herself on many fronts, using this as a rationale for not having enough time or energy to parent her child. As a police officer she chose to work many overtime hours in the child abuse division to help troubled families. Wendy often worked a second job during the Christmas season, and she chose to carry the bulk of the caretaker burden when her parents became sick, even though she herself was chronically ill with multiple sclerosis. Although she has three professionally successful brothers, it was Wendy who assumed most of the family responsibilities. Wendy, in essence, has spent much of her adult life trying to solve the problems of everyone, except her daughter.

According to Karma, she really has not needed much mothering from Wendy. However, there's clearly a great deal of anger that fuels the relationship between the two. For example, Karma displays a classic symptom of children of disengaging parents when her voice, riddled with resentment, hits a high note while recounting how Wendy became the "mother hen" for the entire family (excluding Karma) after her own mother died.

Wendy modeled her behavior after her father, a police officer and a workaholic. Her father spent much free time involved in community service activities focused on needy youth. So, just as Karma on a certain level was abandoned by Wendy, Wendy was abandoned by her father, and the results were predictable. Karma became angry and resentful when Wendy decided to start playing the parental authority role and impose guidelines on her daughter after not being around much for at least 12 years. As Karma grew older, she rebelled with even more vigor against her mother's efforts to behave in a motherly fashion. From Karma's point of view, it was too late for that type of relationship. She refused to go to college and ended up being thrown out of the house. A youthful Wendy had likewise rebelled against her family. She married at 19 against her parent's wishes and dropped out of college. Wendy and Karma have similar histories in one other area: At 19, Karma has already established a pattern of workaholism. She has held down two jobs at the same time since she was 17.

This chapter was particularly difficult for me to write, because it hit so close to home. The most important lesson I learned from examining my own disengaging behavior, along with the experience of this family, is how easy it is to become consumed by self-involvement. I certainly didn't consciously want to abandon my son, but in truth I was so involved with my own struggles to feel okay about myself through gaining the approval of others, I simply became blind to the interests and concerns of the person who needed me the most—my son. My pattern of self-absorption was Wendy's pattern. And the way she behaved was patterned after her father. Whether Wendy's daughter and my son follow in our co-dependent footsteps, however, depends in large part on us as parents, on our willingness to change.

One way to determine if you are a self-involved parent is to look at how you spend your time. List the major activities in your life according to how much time you devote to each of them. Put at the top of the list the activities that take up the most time, then honestly assess who benefits from everything you've listed. Is there a pattern? Are your children proving not to be a high priority in your life?

CHAPTER 7

THE INEFFECTIVE PARENT

My father was an ineffective parent, prone to foisting his adult responsibilities onto the shoulders of his children. He rarely if ever disciplined us. When he and Mother were married that was her responsibility; when they divorced, my sister and brother were in large part expected to raise themselves, though my father maintained legal custody of them until his death. As I've explained earlier, Father was a compulsive gambler who relied on me, his oldest child, to lie to loan sharks who often pounded on our door at all hours to collect the money he owed. As I grew older, there were many times when he expected me to provide him "loans" when he couldn't make ends meet. I became, in other words, his caretaker, his parent of sorts. Often I felt pressured, and sometimes bullied, by my father to accept more responsibilities than I could emotionally or financially handle. Yet for the most part I was compliant because I was afraid. I believed that if I didn't go along with his wishes, he would abandon me. Ironically, I failed to realize that in effect he had already abandoned me by his ineffective parenting.

Generally, my image of my father was that of a kind but weak man. He spoiled us, for example, by finding a way to purchase whatever we requested whether or not the family could afford it. On the other hand, when Mother would discipline me with a belt, his way of helping me was to devise a passive-aggressive strategy for "getting back" at her. "The way to get back at your mother is to not cry when she beats you, no matter how bad it hurts," Father would say when I went to him for solace. Though I followed his advice, even as a nine-year-old child I knew it didn't feel right. I wondered, "If he agrees with me that the beating was unjustified, why won't he defend me and say something to Mom?"

These days, I better understand the dynamics between my parents. Because of Father's heavy gambling losses, he had to depend on Mother's income to support the household, so he deferred to her demands in most matters—except his gambling. He also encouraged my defiant, rebellious behavior as a way of using me to indirectly fight the battles with my mother that he was unwilling to fight himself. So I had a love-hate relationship with my father, though for many years I denied that I resented his manipulation of me. For a long time I believed that it was wrong of me to feel any bad thoughts about my father's ineffectiveness as a parent and the concomitant burdens his behavior imposed upon me as a child and as an adult. My ambivalence, then, caused me to carry around a lot of guilt concerning my father.

It has been 12 years since Father died at age 59 of a sudden heart attack, yet I only recently stopped feeling guilty about the circumstances surrounding his death. By the last year of his life, he was unable to work because of diabetes. Mother had divorced him, and his history of gambling had left him virtually penniless, so I sent him money on a regular basis. Because I was having financial problems right before his death, I had to delay sending a check I had promised. When he died without receiving that check, I felt guilty because I wanted my father to have faith in my intent to support him financially as long as he requested my help. And my guilt was not abated when I found out he had been visiting the racetrack right up until he succumbed to heart failure.

"I CANNOT GIVE YOU WHAT YOU NEED"

Ineffective parents are classically addictive, self-destructive personalities who abandon their children in favor of their addictions. Often these mothers and fathers are substance abusers, but not necessarily. My father's compulsive gambling was another type of addiction. The mother in this chapter's family profile was a love addict—at the expense of her children and in the name of love, she relentlessly and compulsively devoted most of her life to a man who virtually despised her. Basically, such parents are so out of control of their own lives that they are incapable of handling the responsibilities of raising a child. Indeed, it is common for these parents to lean on their children for support and guidance. They are insecure, carry around a lot of self-hatred, and give their sons and daughters the message, "I am overwhelmed. I cannot give you what you need."

This message was clearly demonstrated in my family when my parents ended their marriage. Father gained custody of my 15-year-old sister and 10-year-old brother. I was away at college. Father had a difficult time coping with the breakup of his 25-year marriage, especially since my mother had divorced him for another man. So he immediately positioned my sister to take over the role Mother had vacated. My sister became the disciplinarian for our younger brother, and she was responsible for getting him ready for school. She also had to make the grocery list and plan the meals for the week, as well as offer Father advice on all manner of topics—his divorce and how the family finances should be managed, for example. Taking on such adult responsibilities caused her to feel isolated, scared, confused, and resentful. She began to lose touch with her own identity: "I didn't even know who I was. I was so busy being a surrogate wife for my father, I wasn't connecting with myself." During this period, my sister started using drugs. Today she is a crack cocaine addict.

In a manner typical of most ineffective parents, my father asked his children to assume adult roles that were beyond their emotional capability. Often such children find themselves putting an alcoholic father to bed and telling lies to an employer, other family members, and friends to cover up the parent's addictive behavior. These children also are asked to make key decisions for the parent, such as where the family should live, whether the parent should divorce, or whom the parent should date. Children from these families tend to be very fearful, because there is no safe place for them. They must look after themselves and their parents at a time when they are ill-equipped to take on either responsibility. And if these youngsters make a mistake, they are blamed by their parents. Consequently, they perpetually fear the loss of their parents' approval, which translates in a young person's mind as a loss of parental love. Such children feel trapped, since instead of being protected, guided, and nurtured by their parents, the roles are reversed—they are forced to give to their parents what they as children need but cannot receive.

Just as the sons and daughters of ineffective parents are quite fearful, so are their parents. These mothers and fathers are afraid of how their addictions have taken control of their lives. They are afraid of their inability to take care of themselves and their family. They are afraid of responsibility and they are afraid of losing the respect of their children. To that end, an ever-repeated statement of my dad's was, "You don't have to love me, but as your father I demand your respect." However, like most ineffective parents, my father did not get what he wanted from his child—I always loved him, but I never respected him. As I grew older, though, I tried to understand him.

My father was raised by an ineffective mother who literally abandoned him at an early age. His parents separated when he and his six sisters and brothers were young children. My father was the youngest. They were very poor and lived in a small, run-down apartment. His mother was beautiful and spent a lot of time dating various men. One day when my father was about 13, during the Depression of the 1930s, he returned home from school to find his mother had moved without warning, leaving only a letter for him. The letter explained how she had finally met a man who was willing to take care of her and how she had to look out for herself. She explained that she had left for Philadelphia with this man and ended the letter by asking my father to try to understand her actions. She then wished him good luck in making it on his own. So at 13, in the midst of the Great Depression, my father had to become his own parent.

In addition to being fearful, adult children of ineffective parents typically are insecure and angry, and sometimes display depressive personalities. They are insecure because of the pressure-filled situation they were placed in at such an early age. These children are unsure whether they are making the best decisions for themselves and other family members when they are maneuvered by their parents into accepting responsibilities far beyond their emotional range. As adults, many have a difficult time making decisions, or routinely second-guess the quality of their decisions. They simply don't trust their own judgment.

Virtually all adult children of ineffective parents are angry at their parents for having forced them to become primary caretakers. Some of these adults, however, repress their anger and become depressive personalities. My father, for instance, never admitted he felt any anger toward his mother, but often when discussing her he would clench his teeth and his face would become stiff as granite. He also brooded a lot about his life and displayed a great deal of cynicism. I spent much of my adult life being openly angry at my mother but refusing to acknowledge any anger at my father's behavior, because I saw him as the only friend—no matter how flawed—that I had, given the acrimony that existed between my mother and myself. Still, until I was able to confront the co-dependent shortcomings in my father's personality as I had already done in my mother's and my own personalities, I spent many a night trying to pull myself out of inexplicable depressions. Developing an awareness, then, of how I was hurt by my father's ineffective parenting played an important role in my recovery process.

BECOMING AWARE

Identifying oneself, one's spouse, or one's mother or father as an ineffective parent is for most people a pretty difficult task. I was in my late thirties before I was willing to view my father as a human being who had a flawed character. Growing up, I considered Father my only friend; he nicknamed me his Little Buddy. I was afraid to examine him honestly because I was afraid to alienate him and be left with no one who cared about me. Consequently, I assigned him the false role of hero. For many years I would not let go of that image of him, especially after he died.

It was difficult for me to give up my own self-conceived hero status and identify myself as having been, at times, an ineffective parent. My ineffectiveness spanned a period when I was so unhappy and depressed that I became suicidal and shared in minute detail with my son my feelings of not wanting to live. My son was sent to live with his father, my former husband, until I climbed out of a slump that lasted about four years. Later my son told me that he dreaded hearing the ring of his father's telephone during that time; he expected that it would be someone calling to announce that I was dead. I feel somewhat uncomfortable even now recounting that story. I wish I had not caused my son so much pain. But there is no denying my behavior and my ineffective parenting during that period. These days, however, I find both solace and celebration in my and my son's ability to talk about our past and be healed by the truthfulness of our exchange.

To that end, I encourage you to carefully and honestly read the following list of statements commonly made by ineffective mothers and fathers. Though it will probably be painful for you to acknowledge yourself as having displayed such co-dependent behavior, try to remember the significant opportunity that arises when you accept responsibility for your actions: You have control over, and thus can change, everything for which you are responsible. The list is excerpted from materials prepared for an effective parenting class by teachers from the Hacienda–La Puente School District.

- "I can't take this."
- "What do you think I should do?"
- "I can't talk to him. You do it."
- "I don't know. Ask your dad (mom)."
- "I can't tell your mom, it will upset her."
- "I'm too upset to talk to you."
- "I'll make you pay for this."
- "I hate you."

Ineffective parents, in essence, shift life's responsibilities off themselves and onto someone else—typically their child, sometimes their spouse. They tend to either lash out at their child if pressured into behaving like a parent, or they withdraw from the child even more. A good friend of mine, who cornered her mother 17 years ago about her ineffectiveness as a parent, is still visibly shaken when she recounts her mother's swift and cutting reaction. My friend's mother let her come and go as she pleased—she could stay away for days at a time without asking for permission or even saying where she could be located. When she was about 12 she confronted her mother with her frustration about the way she was being raised. Her mother responded, "I hate you every bit as much as you hate me." My father took the opposite tack. The one time that I mustered up the courage as a child to tell him how I felt about his ineffective behavior, he pulled away and didn't talk to me for about a week.

Jennifer, the 64-year-old mother in this chapter's family profile, withdraws from her children in a less obvious manner when they confront her with her ineffectiveness. On one hand, she virtually encourages her three adult daughters to criticize her ineffective parenting and, for a moment, seems to revel in their negative assessment by agreeing with almost everything they say. But then a protective shield of sorts descends; she appears to detach herself from the conversation and looks as if she is daydreaming. The result is that Jennifer's co-dependent behavior does not change. Indeed, she continues to behave in large part as she did when her daughters were children: She still tries to maneuver 38-year-old Elaine, 35-year-old Kim, and 32-year-old Jody into taking care of her emotionally, a task that Dan, Jennifer's husband of 30 years, was unwilling to do.

Jennifer married a man with whom she was desperately in love but who did not love her. She spent approximately 30 years trying to win his adoration. In fact, making Dan happy became an obsession that ultimately took precedence over the raising of her daughters, particularly Elaine, who was the apple of her father's eye.

Dan died four years ago, thus he could not provide testimony for this profile. Jennifer, Elaine, Kim, and Jody were interviewed at length. All were fairly candid, though Kim was reluctant to let certain statements remain on the record for fear that her comments would hurt the feelings of other family members. Jennifer, on the other hand, was quick to provide proof of her cooperative spirit by announcing early on in the interview that I could count on her to tell the truth because Elaine had instructed her to do so—a directive she never issued, Elaine asserts.

FAMILY PROFILE:

Jennifer, Elaine, Kim, and Jody

Jennifer, 64, is a pleasant woman who has spent much of her life unsure of herself. She tends to ask the most mundane questions of everyone around her to determine how to handle any problem—large or small. Indeed, Jennifer is an adult who acts very much like a little girl. Consequently, she has leaned on her daughters for emotional support and guidance since they were children. In particular she has relied on them to help her overcome the heartaches derived from one of the few decisions she did make on her own and of which she was initially very confident: marrying Dan.

Jennifer fell in love with Dan after moving to Brooklyn when she was about 17. It was love at first sight—for her. Dan had to be "pursued" by Jennifer to convince him to marry her. Though he agreed to the marriage, he never returned her love. Jennifer's pursuit of Dan's affection continued throughout their 30-year marriage. She placed the winning of his love above all else. She admits, "I was not there for my children. Dan came first."

Jennifer never ranked as high with Dan, however. He ultimately divorced her to marry a woman with whom he had conducted a 10-year affair. Prior to walking away from the marriage, Dan routinely spoke to his wife in a demeaning manner and rarely valued her input. Jennifer's undying love in the face of Dan's abuse has engendered a great deal of anger toward her from her daughters. They wanted her to stand up for herself, to demand respect. When their father left, they considered it the best thing that could have happened to their mother. At first, Jennifer says, "I resented that, because that was *not* the best thing. The best thing was if he had stayed with me." These days, she says she agrees with her daughters. But given the way Jennifer second-guesses herself, a listener is left in some doubt as to whether she really means what she says.

Jennifer lives alone in New York. Elaine and Jody reside in Los Angeles; Kim lives in Arizona. Elaine, 38, and Kim, 35, are married; Jody, 32, is not. Neither daughter has children. Elaine says she is simply not interested in having a child. Kim wants children, but health problems have thus far prevented her from having a son or daughter. Jody wants a family when the right man comes along and the timing is right. All of the daughters still evince anger toward their mother, though Kim is a little less forthcoming about such feelings. These three women also are preoccupied with their co-dependent upbringing and spend a lot of time talking to each other to analyze what happened in their household, to sort out the impact their upbringing has had on their lives.

Jennifer

At first blush, Jennifer appears to be a happy person. She has a playful sense of humor, yet her good cheer belies a sadness and regret that are evident from the moment she begins telling her story. "I only knew my father 17 years, because he died when I was 17. I always said I lost my friend, not my father. He understood me. I got along with him and I loved him very much." Jennifer was one of three children. Her older brother was revered by her father; her younger sister was adored by everyone. Though Jennifer loved her two siblings, she harbored some resentment toward them, which occasionally exploded into fights. She felt pretty good about herself away from home, she says, because "I owned my block. In other words, I had both of my parents for a while, my father owned a grocery store, we lived in an apartment above his store, and I always had a sense of security. We were never in want even during the Depression."

One downside of Jennifer's upbringing was that she was protected, especially by her father's notions of what women should or should not do. "I was never allowed to go to college, because I was a girl. Girls were supposed to get married and not have to go to college. And this was the big thing that I held against my parents, though I understood where my father was coming from. He never understood the American way of sending your children to college. My parents were from Austria and he had had to quit school at the age of five. So he never really went to school yet he ran a successful business." Jennifer's mother acquiesced to her father's belief that his daughters should go to work, meet a fellow, and get married.

In this regard, what her parents wanted for her, Jennifer did not want for her own children. "I decided when I got married that whether I had girls or boys, they were going to college and then going away, so that they would become independent, because I was very dependent on my parents all of these years. I think if I was 30 and never married I still wouldn't have moved out on my own, because in my parents' house this was not the way it was done."

As an afterthought, Jennifer criticizes herself. "I saw my friends from school go on to college, while I wanted to and should have, and I could have gone at night, but I didn't because there was no incentive, no push, and I didn't have the wherewithal within myself to do these things—which is my fault. But why couldn't I?" Jennifer's answer to her own question involves her father. He died of a heart attack right after she graduated from high school, which changed her life in ways that left her too insecure to branch out on her own. "I was very, very unhappy during those years. I think it took me about three years to get over my father's death. I was a basket case. I didn't get along that well with my mother. We fought a lot. So, if anything happened to me, my father would be there to comfort me, although when my father died, my mother would give me material things and try to make it up to me that I didn't have a father."

Jennifer also engaged in a lot of fights with her sister and brother. "I was jealous of my sister because she was such a nice, cute girl. She became a very quiet, reserved lady. And when I say a lady, I mean lady. And I was jealous of my brother because he was my mother's favorite. I'm the middle child and I was not appreciated at home. I always got into trouble at home, but I loved school. I was appreciated there. So I used to hate Saturdays and Sundays." Often her father would hear fights between Jennifer and her brother over which radio programs they would listen to. "My brother would throw me against the wall from one end of the room to the other. My father would come and throw the radio out of the window to settle the fight." But the next day, he would buy another radio.

Still, Jennifer recalls, "No one cried as hard as I did when my brother left for the army. I was about 16, and you would have thought that I was saying goodbye to my husband. I remember crying bitterly when he left, because I really loved him." But, she adds, foretelling the type of relationship she would have with her husband, "My brother loved my sister and I didn't think he loved me." Jennifer believes that she was unloved by her brother because she was fat. "He never liked fat women. So he loved my sister because she always was thin." Likewise, one of Dan's complaints against Jennifer was her being overweight.

Her marriage also was influenced by the example set by her parents. "My father came first. My mother had a saying, 'You take care of yourself, and you take care of your husband, and then the children will get what's coming to them.' In other words, my mother lived for my father." Jennifer distorted this model of behavior, however, when she applied it to her own marriage, because she left out the first step and barely connected with the third. She adopted a more extreme and selective version of her mother's philosophy, because of the way she observed her mother-in-law mistreat her spouse in favor of Dan and her other children. "My mother-in-law lived for her children at the exclusion of her husband, and

I wasn't going to do that because I thought that the way she treated her husband was terrible. I thought my mother-in-law was a dominating person and my father-in-law was a nothing."

Jennifer "adored" her prospective husband, however. "I loved him from the first day I met him. While he was a month older than me, he was 10 years older in terms of his maturity. He was very...introverted, that's the word for him. He was very intelligent and I thought he was good looking. We were only about 16 or 17 when we met and I would hang around with him, but I don't think he had the attraction toward me that I had toward him. So I would say that I pursued him."

When Dan went into the army, she got engaged to somebody else, but broke that off when Dan returned from overseas. Jennifer's assessment of why Dan agreed to marry her despite his obvious lack of earnest affection for her, has to do with his dysfunctional family life. "I think he wanted to get out of his family situation. He was sleeping in the living room. They were poor people, and I think that he just wanted to get married and have his own home." Jennifer and Dan were 23 when they married.

Jennifer believed that Dan was strong, someone to lean on. "I can't say I married a father figure, I didn't marry someone who was five or ten years older than me, but I was so flighty and immature that I thought he was so much smarter and so much more mature." Much to Jennifer's surprise, once she married Dan, he turned out to be a weak, nervous person. "He was depressed a lot and he had something physically wrong with him that wasn't diagnosed for many years." At about age 40, it was determined that Dan had fibrillation of the heart, which is sometimes caused by rheumatic fever. He suffered a great deal of anxiety over his undiagnosed illness, because he was a sportsman who enjoyed physical activity. Jennifer recalls, "I'd take him to see doctors and they'd say, 'Go home. You're in physically fine health.'" Dan eventually had a nervous breakdown, for which he was hospitalized.

"Because of his nervousness, I was very protective of him, and this is where my children lost out. They didn't have a mother. I worried about him and tried to protect him from feeling too much. I didn't want him to feel pressured." When Elaine was born, for example, Dan had an anxiety attack.

"He never, never looked happy and he was always trying to escape. He would play golf. He would say, 'I'm sick. I have to go out and play. I have to relax.' So I fell into a pattern of protecting him. I loved him and there was nobody in this world who meant more to me. And I explained that to the children. I said, 'I'm a lucky girl that he still loves me.' He simply meant everything to me—to the exclusion of my mother, my children, anybody. Everyone knew how much I loved him, but no one would say, 'He loves you.'

"I could never win his love. I could never do anything that would please him. And the more he was the way he was, the less loving I became of myself. My children recognized it, because when he left me, my middle child said, 'That's the best thing that could happen to you.'"

She knew he was going to leave, Jennifer recalls, because "he had removed himself from our home a long time before he left. He went to play golf. Then he took up painting, and I never felt that he wanted to be home with his family and his children. He was always escaping." Dan also used his oldest daughter to distance himself from Jennifer. "When I gave birth to Elaine it was like giving birth to Jesus Christ. My husband adored her. I remember she was 13 months old and I tried to explain to him that I felt neglected. But he said that Elaine came first. When she was older, if she got angry and ran up to her room, I would want to go up to her and comfort her and talk it out with her, but he wouldn't let me. He would say, 'I'll go.' And to this day I still feel guilty about not insisting that I go. I've said to Elaine as an adult, 'I'm so sorry that I wasn't strong enough to tell Dan, "I want to go up. You stay down."'" Because she did not take a stand, Dan and Elaine developed a relationship of which Jennifer was jealous.

Her ineffectiveness also extended to Kim and Jody because, Jennifer says, "If I had had a loving husband, I could have been more loving. Elaine has a home movie of me where I'm undressing her on her bed and she says that I'm staring off into space in order to escape my thoughts. Elaine says, 'I never felt you were there for me.' If I had had a different kind of husband, would I have been a different kind of mother? Could I have given more love?"

Jennifer remembers that "everything I did was for him. I was so sad when Elaine left for college, because I felt badly for him. Not for me, but for him. I thought, 'He's going to lose Elaine.' I went to a psychiatrist right after he left and after talking to me he said, 'You're the kind of person who if you love somebody will put yourself down as a doormat.' And that's what I did with Dan. I said to this therapist, 'I hope I meet a man and prove you wrong, because if I don't prove you wrong, I'm going to commit suicide, because I don't think I could live the way I lived with Dan.'"

Jennifer describes her life with Dan as having been divided into two stages: before and after his nervous breakdown. He was in psychoanalysis for seven years and, according to Jennifer, "He emerged a different kind of person, who I didn't like as much as I liked before." He became more assertive and more self-assured. The more aggressive he became, the more she withdrew. "He sucked the blood and guts out of me and I became something I didn't like. I became something different."

As her personality became more timid and even more subservient to her husband, her relationship with her daughters deteriorated. Also, her own mother was displeased with Jennifer's behavior, especially her insistence on working for Dan, who was an accountant. Jennifer, in fact, still feels guilty about how on the night her mother died, she was more interested in taking care of Dan's business concerns than tending to her mother's dead body and her children's fears.

"It was a traumatic thing. My mother died in my [New York] house babysitting while I was in New Jersey working with my husband on an audit. It was near New Year's Eve when she died at the top of the stairs and fell down. My little girl heard it, my children were all there and my brother-in-law and his wife were there. My mother was sleeping in the same room with my youngest daughter, who heard her get up and cry out and fall down the stairs, but my youngest daughter never got up. The noise shook the lamps in the living room where another child was sleeping on the couch, and that's where I found my mother—dead at the foot of the steps. Of course, all of my children were affected by it, but I was worried about typing up the notes I had written earlier for my husband's client. I was worried that Dan and his client wouldn't be able to understand my shorthand, so while the police were at the house and my mother was lying dead, I was typing. So can you picture what I mean when I say my husband came first to the exclusion of my mother and my children?"

As the years passed, Jennifer and Dan became estranged. Dan starting seeing another woman and eventually, after a 10-year affair, divorced Jennifer to marry her. Jennifer responded to the further downturn in her marriage by becoming more and more detached from her family, particularly her children. "I was off playing tennis with all of the free time that I had. That was what I did. My husband never allowed me near Elaine, so I'm not close to her. The other ones [Kim and Jody] I knew, because they were around a little more." Jennifer rarely confronted Dan with her anger and resentment. "I thought to myself, 'All of the love that I had for you is just gone.' Yet I was willing to settle for being Mrs. _____, because of my way of life. I didn't have a husband, per se, because we were like strangers. But I wouldn't tell him what I thought, because I didn't want to confront him. No one wanted to confront him, because he could talk circles around you and then reject you. I would feel very upset when I had a fight with him. He wouldn't talk for a week. He'd stay angry and I couldn't take it. So it was easier not to fight and to give in. And as you give in, you lose your credibility, you lose your sense of who you are, and that's what happened. My children saw that, they saw that I wouldn't stand up for them. So what do you think of a mother who wasn't there for you?"

Elaine, her oldest child, still does not respect Jennifer. She still reminds her mother of how bad a parent she was. "Sometimes Elaine will say, 'Oh, I hurt myself.' So, I'll say, 'You really should go see a doctor,' and Elaine will cut me short and start yelling at me in a nasty tone, 'You weren't a mother before, what are you going to be, a mother now?' And she's right. But I'm not trying to be like a mother, I'm just giving advice. But she takes it like that.

"Elaine does not accept anything I say. A lot of times I don't understand her. But I respect her. I have a different relationship with my middle child. Kim is a much warmer person than Elaine. Maybe she's not as honest, but she knows what to say to you, and everybody thinks she's so fantastic because she's sweet, loving, kind, and good. Whether it's true or not, this is the way Kim comes across. Elaine doesn't think Kim is honest. But Kim accepts me, and I can't understand why Elaine can't accept me like Kim does. Kim gets angry at me and she'll tell me off, but I can take it from her. I can't take it from Elaine. And Jody, the little one, is getting to be just like Elaine."

Jennifer's relationship with her daughters has changed very little over the years, because she is still struggling with many of the same codependent patterns of behavior she displayed during their upbringing. She doesn't call her children often, because it's easier not to interact with them. "What am I going to talk to them about? So I don't call them every week, because I haven't got anything to say to them. They don't call me that often, either." Jennifer also continues to attract men who treat her as Dan did. "I contend I loved Dan enough for two. But now I want to be loved. Yet, I could have married a man who wanted to marry me and who I could see was a very loving and caring man with his first wife. He would have been that way with me. He would have given me anything I want, but he wasn't my type. Is it that I don't like that type of person? Is it that I am attracted to the ones who are cold toward me?"

After pausing for a moment, Jennifer answers her own question. "I think that's the type of man I'm attracted to, the type that treats me badly. That's why I don't seek relationships these days. I find it very hard to get involved. After my divorce from Dan, I got involved with a man who was not all that giving in a lot of ways, but I was attracted to him. And when we broke up, I felt very badly, yet I knew it would never be a long-lasting relationship, because he didn't want to get married. We had a very odd relationship. I'd only see him on Thursday nights because he had his club on the weekends and I had my tennis club on the weekends. Finally, he went back to an old girlfriend and we broke off. I felt bad, but I was also grateful to this man, because until I got involved with him, there was never another man on earth but my husband. I was thankful that this man helped me know that I was able to feel some emotion for someone other than Dan."

Still, Jennifer has many regrets. "I wish I could meet a nice man I was attracted to instead of cold men, so that I could prove the psychiatrist wrong. But I don't know that that will happen. I'm sorry that for 30 years I lived a very unloving life. But that is, in essence, my life. Yet, if I had had a different type of husband I know I would have been a different type of mother, and we would have been more of a family. And this is what makes me sad."

Elaine

Elaine, 38, is articulate and thoughtful about her relationship with her parents. She is also angry at both of them.

"My father is the only one I remember being with me and taking care of me. He used to give me a bath. He used to comb my hair. My mother, really, was not there for me. I felt she didn't like me, that she didn't like when my father and I were together. I remember when I was about seven or eight years old, I was standing in the hall one day when my mother and father were there and my mother walked over to him and twined her arms around him and gave him a long, lingering kiss. He just stood there and stiffened. I remember getting really sick inside and saying to myself, 'Don't you know he doesn't love you?' So I suspected that she didn't like me because my father liked me and he didn't like her."

Dan's attitude toward Elaine altered after his nervous breakdown, which caused problems between father and daughter, but Jennifer's and Elaine's relationship appears to have been consistent—they have shared very little over the years. "After my father had a nervous breakdown he sort of withdrew. I remember when I was about 12 or 13 being really angry at my father, I remember our not getting along. But my mother never entered the picture. From when I was a little girl to the time my mother and father got divorced, we had basically no relationship."

If she wasn't around to be a mother, where was Jennifer? Elaine recalls, "She was very tomboyish. She would play football with the guys on the block. She was very, very outgoing. But to me it was a shrill sort of outgoing. There was something that wasn't quite real about it and it used to bother me. She'd always criticize me for being shy. She'd tell me to get out there and do things, but I kept thinking to myself, 'I don't want to be like you.' So we had an antagonistic relationship when I was growing up. But not overtly antagonistic."

On the other hand, despite Dan's behavioral swing away from Elaine after his breakdown, she still felt a strong identification with him. "He scared me because I knew there was something different about my father's behavior. I felt that he was really unhappy. And what happened was, as I got older I was unhappy, too. But he couldn't help me because he was so sunk in whatever he was going through. I remember when I was in high school, I suddenly got terrified that I was going to flunk and that I was going to be a failure. Out of the blue I became terrified. I think part of it was that my family was not a secure place to be, so I never felt like I had anyplace to go. I was ending high school, preparing to go off to college to face the unknown, and I was feeling afraid to leave home. I applied to a college in Chicago, although I was terrified to leave home, because somehow I knew I had to get away."

Elaine's identification with her father was nurtured by Dan. "After my father died of cancer, I was terrified that I would die of cancer too because my whole life my father kept telling me how much alike we were. He would tell me about his life and how unhappy he was and how anxiety-ridden he was, and he tried to identify with me in really unhealthy ways. It got me very, very upset and I sort of wanted to push him away." At one point, in fact, Elaine did not speak to her father for about two and a half years.

"My parents divorced when I was 29, and about one year later I just fell apart. I had a lot of anxiety, and I decided to go into therapy. When I was in therapy I began exploring my past, and at that point I became angry at my father. He called up one day and started chatting away, when I said, 'Dad, I can't talk to you now. I know this isn't fair, but I'm really angry about all of the things that you did to me when I was a kid and I'm going to work through it. Don't worry about it, but I don't want to talk now.' He said, 'Okay,' and hung up. About two minutes later the phone rang and he said, 'If you don't know why you're angry at me, I know why I'm angry at you.' He proceeded to tell me how ungrateful I was and about everything I'd done to him for the past 29 years. Then he said, 'So when you figure out whatever is bothering you, you call me,' and hung up. So we ended up not talking for about two and a half years, and then one of my sisters told me that he had cancer. I called him to tell him that I was sorry and ask if we could see one another."

Elaine flew to New York, where her father was having an operation, to effect a reconciliation. She admits that it wasn't a complete success. "It has been a little over three years since he died. This year I was lighting a mourning candle for the anniversary of his death, and I looked at my husband and said, 'Well, the only thing I'm going to get out of this is a juice glass.' In my family, we always used empty mourning candle containers for juice glasses. Then I called my sisters the next day and said, 'This is really horrible, but I'm glad he's not here.' I have to say at this point that I feel much better now that I don't have to deal with him in any way."

Elaine's push-pull relationship with her father and virtual nonexistent relationship with her mother have affected her in many ways, particularly in her associations with females. "For years I had trouble in friendships with women. I felt much more comfortable with men. All through my college years and into my early twenties, I had women friends, but sort of trivial women friends. Then when I went into therapy, I picked a woman therapist, because I figured that would help. Soon, I went through this wonderful stage in my life where I would just leap on any woman who wanted to be my friend. So I had a lot of stupid women friends. But then I decided I would just find people who matter in my life. Now I have a lot of regular relationships with women, but I think my problem with women had to do with my mother. We just never did anything together. Never. She never even taught me how to brush my teeth. Whenever I got upset, the only person who would comfort me was my father. I never had a woman role model."

Jennifer, it seems, simply stayed on the sidelines of Elaine's life. "My mother was sort of spacy. I have some home movies of me when I was about two or three, sitting on the bed. My mother's supposed to be dressing me. But I've gotten myself tangled up and I'm rolling around on the bed and my mother—the camera is on both of us—is just looking off into space somewhere. It's like she's not even there. And it's the weirdest look. It's sort of scary."

Dan's role as Elaine's primary comforter, on the other hand, was not all it appeared to be. "My father and I would sit and whine together. He would totally identify with me, especially if I was feeling full of anxiety. He wouldn't help me get out of a bad mood, he would get me in deeper because he would identify with my down-and-out feelings. So I grew up with a sense of doom. I remember that when I was happy or excited about some good news, my father would say, 'If today is good, tomorrow is going to be lousy.' I grew up with this really negative belief that something bad was always about to happen. I spent a lot of my life looking behind myself and worrying—and I still have that tendency, which I really hate. Of course there are going to be ups and downs in life, but my father lived in the downs all of the time, and I've had to learn how to fight that tendency."

Elaine also has had to learn how to communicate with her mother, which has been difficult, given their history. "One thing that I have had to struggle with in my life is being too honest, because of all of the lies that went on in my family. I decided when I was 17 that I would never tell a lie. My mother lies even when she knows that you know she's lying, which is totally frustrating. I think what she does is tell people what she thinks they want to hear."

From time to time, Jennifer cannot figure out what to say to please the person to whom she is talking. When that happens, Jennifer shifts into another mode of behavior, which causes Elaine to become even more frustrated. "Sometimes my mother says exactly the wrong thing. It's amazing. And it has reached the point that I don't feel like I should tell her things that really matter, because I don't get the support I need. She doesn't know what to say. She literally needs me to tell her how she should respond. And who wants to tell somebody something and then say, 'Now Mom, I don't want you to say anything. I just want you to listen and every now and then tell me that you understand.' In other words, to have to tell somebody how to react is not having them react at all."

Elaine attributes her mother's behavior to the fact that Jennifer has spent much of her life refusing to acknowledge her feelings—particularly feelings of anger—and that that repression has led to an overwhelming sadness in her mother and occasional vindictiveness. "Once my mother called me, after my father's death, to ask me why I hadn't talked to him during about a three-year period. She said, 'Well, you were always so close. He would always go up to your room and would never let me up there. He would take care of you. And now I read all of this stuff about incest and child abuse and I wonder what was going on up there.'

"I got so sick to my stomach, I just sat down in the middle of the kitchen floor. I got her off the phone abruptly and just burst into tears, and my husband came in and comforted me. Then I went grocery shopping and started crying in the checkout line. When I got home it was 11 P.M., which is 2 A.M. in New York, but I thought, 'I have to call my mother.' I called her and said, 'I don't ever want to talk to you again if you instill poison like this in my mind. If you are angry at my father, don't lay it on me. You can say that you hate my father and that's fine. I can help you with that. But I can't do it when it's directed at me. And I'm not going to take this from you.' We had a good cry together and got off the phone, but I realized she's going to be angry at me because she can't be angry at my father. I also think my mother is really unhappy. So a while ago, I went on a crusade to say to her, 'You're unhappy, you're unhappy. Admit it.'" Elaine's method of helping her mother see the light was to no avail. Now she is trying to let go of her own need to "cure" her mother.

"I'm trying to get to the place where I can accept that my mother is not going to suddenly become a different person. I'm trying to figure out a way of interacting with her so that I can get off the phone [after talking to her] and feel good about myself. I go through different stages with her. Sometimes she really gets to me, because, number one, I can feel her unhappiness, which is painful for me and I can't change the way she feels. Number two, I feel her antagonism, which I don't like to feel either. So it's still sort of a love-hate thing with the two of us."

Elaine's relationship with her sisters has also been rocky over the years. "My sister Jody came to Los Angeles to visit me from New York about seven years ago, before she moved out here, and we had a great time together. Toward the end of the visit she said, 'You know, I really like you. You're not at all like Dad says you are.' I was surprised and asked her, 'What do you mean?' Jody said, 'We'd have these family meetings in the den and he'd go on and on about how cold and uncaring you are.' Here I was, trying to live my own life and be happy, which was a struggle, and to have my family on the East Coast saying, 'She's horrible, she's cold,' which I felt wasn't true, really hurt me."

As recently as a couple of years ago, the anger toward Elaine was still evident in her middle sister, Kim. "Not too long ago, we had a family reunion around Christmastime at Kim's place in Arizona. The family re-union was a disaster, at least for Jody and me. I was feeling depressed because I had hurt my leg and I wasn't working and I was worried about what I was going to do with my life. So I tended to keep to myself. Jody told me that when I wasn't in the room Kim and others would start saying, 'Oh, Elaine is this and Elaine is that.' Basically, when I wasn't there, they would be really nasty about me. But when I was there it was a different story.

"Kim and my mother are angry with me for being me, for daring to be selfish—at least that's how they would describe the way I live my life. And Kim is particularly hard on me about the way I insist our mother should stay in a hotel when she comes to visit. She thinks that I abuse our mother.

Yet, the funny thing is that Kim tells me when she gets off the phone with our mother, her husband says to her, 'How can you treat your mother like this?' And she says, 'Well, that was a rather nice conversation!' "

Because of Elaine's on-and-off-again relationship with her family, she has had periods when she experienced "free-floating anxiety, this formless feeling where I was just terrified. When this happened I felt like I was hurtling somewhere, like I had absolutely no solid place, that I wasn't secure anywhere. I've been through several of these periods—once when I was growing up, and then when I was in college, and the year after my parents got divorced. That was when I thought, 'I've got to get some help.' So now I'm really happy, not that I've worked through everything in my life, but I am more aware of why I've been through all of that anxiety. Some of it had to do with just being in situations where nothing is really real, where there is so much dishonesty. Though I am happy, it has been a gradual process. I didn't suddenly become happy and I'm not insanely, idiotically happy, but I feel like everything has evened out in my life. It's been a long haul."

Has coming to some peace with herself translated into helping her cope with her relationship with her mother? Elaine explains: "The only thing that I know to do is to try to keep the communication as honest as I can between us. I have sort of gotten to the point where I can laugh at something she says and say, 'Do you realize what you're saying?' Also, sometimes she'll try to tell me what I should do and it used to drive me crazy. I used to say to her, 'I can take better care of myself than you can.' But now I say, 'Mom, I think I've done okay for myself. You really don't have to worry about me.' So, I'm learning. My mother never learned to grow up. She's still a little girl in a lot of ways. But I'm learning that that doesn't take away from the fact that in her own way she loves me."

Kim

Kim, 35, is married and resides in Arizona. Her testimony was at times puzzling. She's pleasant and, on the face of it, straightforward, yet she has a blunt way of making statements and understatements that don't always ring true. Her description of whether she was loved by her parents is a case in point. "I spent most of my time outside my family to get warmth and support because my mother spent most of her time trying to please my father to no avail and very little time with us. She did spend some time with Jody, though, but it was a kind of tug-of-war. My father really loved Elaine, so my mother said, 'Well, I'm going to love Jody.' But I didn't feel unloved. I never did because I have an uncle who was single up until I was

11, so he used to come over all of the time, and I remember spending a lot of time with him."

Kim also remembers being raised by a mother whom she describes as a "nothing." "I just look at my mother as being a nothing. When I was a teenager, I'd ask her if I could do something and she'd say, 'I can't answer. Wait until your father gets home.' Or, if she actually gave me an answer and I didn't like the answer, my father would always give me a different answer and that's the answer that would count." Still, Kim says, "I don't think my mother was a bad mother, but she wasn't really good. When I think of mothers, she does not come to my mind. The mother on 'Little House on the Prairie' [a television program] comes to mind, or my friend's mother will come to mind, but not my mother."

Kim's view of her father is different but no less conflicted. "My father was very, very critical, particularly of his family. Superficially I got along with him. It was my choice to get along with him. But when I was a teenager, we did not get along at all. I rebelled by using drugs and sex. Most of the time he ignored my behavior. Every once in a while, when I'd do something really bad, he'd feel guilty and bring home flowers. But most of the time when he ignored me it meant that he was very angry." What constituted an example of "really bad" behavior? "One time I overdosed [on drugs]. I guess that's pretty bad. When I did that he was really nice for a while. He brought me flowers every night, which is something he never did. I assume that he was trying to make himself feel better also, because he spent so much time outside the house."

Kim later discovered that the reason her father was seldom home was that he was having an affair. The way he chose to first hide and then acknowledge that affair has had a long-lasting negative effect on Kim's psyche. "When my mother would go out, he would call Lisa [his girlfriend] on the phone, and if I'd go pick up one of the extension phones to call a friend, all of a sudden people would hang up. And then he'd either come upstairs or I'd come downstairs and we'd play the game, 'How's the weather?' or, 'So what's going on?' As I got older I used to do the same thing when I would lie to my parents about where I was going. I'd come home that night and say, 'So how was your evening?'

"So I suspected for a while that something was going on, and I think part of the reason I started doing drugs and all that is my father started spending so much time away from home. And my parents fought a lot. So although I didn't exactly know what was happening, I used drugs to deal with the strangeness in the house. Then one day I heard him on the phone, heard a conversation with her [Lisa] and he was talking about love and how he didn't know if he knew what love was. I remember going to my friend's house and saying, 'Oh, I think my father is having an affair.' I was upset. I came home and confronted him with it that evening, and he admitted having an affair but said that he wasn't having any more of them."

Her father did not make good his promise. In fact, when he broke the news to her mother sometime later that he was leaving for another woman, Kim was present. "He was in the hospital and my mother and I were visiting and he just kind of blurted it out, 'I can't live with you anymore. I want a divorce.' I was genuinely happy for both of them, because my mother and father were so miserable together that I figured, 'Well, if both of you can't be happy at least one of you can.' For a long time my mother was very angry at me because she believed I had taken my father's side since I had agreed with him about getting a divorce. My mother didn't want a divorce. But what I saw was a man who didn't really like his wife, a man who had spent 30 years with a woman he didn't love, and because of that we were never a family."

Kim feels history supports her decision to favor her father's choice to get a divorce. "My mother has definitely become a happier person since the divorce, because she sees that people like her for herself and not for being Dan's wife. She realizes she can stand alone. Now that he's dead, she feels like she's more of a widow than a divorcee. So she's happier. But she still hasn't changed much. She was in therapy for a little while, until the doctor started asking questions, and then she stopped. My mother's really good at playing her game, and I think that when it started getting difficult she backed out. I probably would have, too, if I were her because her life was so unhappy and because she thinks that her life is just about over, so to find out all of these things is just too painful for her."

However, what Jennifer would not confront with her therapist, her daughters have forced her to confront, or at least hear. According to Kim, Jennifer is "really good at listening" to her daughters' dissatisfaction with their upbringing, but taking action to change is another matter. "I tend to blame my father more for everything than my mother because I can talk to her now about things...well, actually, say things at her is more like it. She understands what I'm saying to her, still sometimes she doesn't get it. She'll agree with what I say, but she's a real good yes-man." Kim pauses, then says, "My mother will never change."

While visiting Elaine and Jody, Jennifer recently agreed to an arrangement that Kim is positive hurt her mother's feelings. Elaine and Jody insisted that Jennifer, who had traveled from New York to Los Angeles expressly to see them, stay at a hotel rather than at either of their homes.

"They wanted to have a good time with her and felt that if she was around all of the time, she would get on their nerves and everyone would end up unhappy. I have to accept that, although I don't particularly like it for my mother, but I'm not my mother's keeper. Still, it hurts me. When my mother visits me, she stays here. She'll get on my nerves and I will yell at her, probably, but I can take it for three or four days. I think it would be more hurtful for me to say to her, 'You have to stay in a hotel because I can't put up with you for four days.' "

On the other hand, Kim doesn't hesitate to state that her mother "really had no input most of my life. So I can say I never want to be like my mother, because my mother was never really there." In the same conversation, however, Kim identifies with her mother in a significant way. Indeed, she differentiates herself from her sisters by describing how her character favors her mother's. "I'm more like my mother. I'm always so concerned about other people's feelings. I'm not selfless by any sense of the word, but I'm less selfish than either one of them [her sisters]. I don't know if that's good or bad. But I tend to worry about people and I tend to be a little more concerned than I need to be. Also, in the case of my mom and even with my father, I knew that I couldn't change them, so I had to accept them and do things that I didn't want to do, but I did it because I didn't want to cause any waves." It is no surprise, then, that Kim admits that she and her sisters are not really close. "As adults we're friends, but the only thing we have in common is the fact that we spend a lot of time talking about our parents and how we were and why we're the way we are.

"I was so unhappy growing up that being unhappy was the norm, and I tend to feel that it's not normal to be happy all of the time. So, although my life is fairly happy right now, I can't accept it as the norm. I always have to question it. To feel normal I have to feel unhappy. I'm trying to sort out a lot of things. I'm still working out my problems because of my upbringing. I have problems with my self-confidence and in making decisions —I'm afraid."

Nevertheless, Kim states that she has resolved most of the important issues with her mother that have bothered her over the years, although there are times when her mother is an irritant. "My mother is annoying. When we're together she takes on the role of the child and I'm the parent. She'll ask a lot of questions—questions that a child would ask an adult— and not even care to hear the answers. It's very annoying. And this summer when I was depressed, my mother sympathized with my husband. I said to her, 'Listen to you. You're still doing it, you're still sympathizing with the man. Poor Steve what? I'm the one who's doing shitty.' But she was so much more concerned with my husband—just as she was with my father—and that really blew me away." Such behavior on Jennifer's part spurs old feelings in Kim of not being loved. Indeed, Kim confesses that if she could have whispered one bit of advice in Jennifer's ear when she first started mothering, it would have been, "Care about your children."

Jody

At 32, Jody recently enrolled in a clinical psychology program. She intends to eventually obtain a Marriage and Family Counselor Certification to help others recover from the negative consequences of co-dependent parenting. She was led to this profession by her own troublesome upbringing. As the youngest of three daughters, Jody was the only one still living at home during the last few years of her parents' marriage, so she saw and heard the worst of Jennifer's and Dan's beleaguered 30-year attempt to live together. Consequently, Jody provides an even harsher view of her parents' relationship than do her sisters.

"My mother basically had no sense of herself. She was ineffective in being there for us kids and for my father, in spite of his being her first priority. She was ineffective for him because when you go to a person and you begin to relate to him as you think he might want you to relate to him, you're mirroring what he wants you to be. And, after a while, you become ineffective because you're no challenge to that person. In essence, the other person is just coming up against himself."

Jody also has an assessment of why her mother was so ineffective as a parent and wife. "I don't think she ever developed a really good self-esteem and a mature attitude toward life. She never became an adult. I categorize her as a chameleon, because she will say things to you that she thinks you want to hear. When we grew up, she was a compulsive liar. She would lie about the stupidest things. For example, one Thanksgiving we knew that she had bought a turkey that was precooked. So I asked her, 'Is this a precooked turkey? It's really good.' She said, 'No. I cooked it myself.' She would just lie about stupid things. Maybe that was her sense of humor, but it just stated to me that she really didn't want to be honest about what she did and who she was. A lot of times when I went to her, I couldn't trust the answers she gave me. And because she had such a terrible relationship with my father, I did not seek her advice because I really didn't respect it."

Through her husband's eyes, Jennifer couldn't do anything right. Through Jody's eyes, Jennifer was wrong all of the time only because she was weak and would not stand up to her husband. "My father set up the family so that everybody had a problem but him. It wasn't his responsibility that everybody had problems, they just had to deal with it. He was very critical and demanding and expected everybody to do what he wanted. And my mother set it up that that was supposed to be true, because she lived for him. He was very emotionally abusive to her, so she didn't stand her ground and say, 'You're not right,' or, 'This is not the way I want to conduct my life.' Instead, she basically caved in to him. I think it was because she didn't have a sense of herself and she was too scared to go after that, to search for herself. And she was scared of losing him. But in the end, she lost him anyway."

Using the clinical psychology jargon that Jody has picked up from her college studies, she describes her father: "He was a classic narcissist. He would do things and if you did not appreciate what he did, he would hit the roof. He wanted respect and he thought love was obligation. In fact, he would do things out of obligation so that you would love and respect him. He didn't do things because he wanted to. And that kind of behavior has a whole different focus on it, it skews everything to a negative.

"My father supported me through college, and I really appreciated that. But when it came down to it, he wanted my life. He wanted to be able to control what I did and how I did it, and I just couldn't give that to him. So he used to get very frustrated, because when he wanted things, he wanted them without any questions asked. I'm my own person and I needed to ask questions, and my father didn't want me to explore anything. My mother just yessed him to death. My mother's response was, 'Okay, okay. You want to do this. That's fine.' She never challenged him."

Jody admits, however, that she, too, didn't challenge her father as much as she should have. "Kim was the rebel in that she involved herself in a lot of rebellious activities. And I think she did it to get attention, to get his love. Elaine was his favorite daughter and he was very attentive to her. I was my mother's daughter and he did not really pay much attention to me. I look like my mother, so physically I was her clone and my father did not like the way my mother looked. She was fat and I was a fat kid. So my self-image was wrapped up with my mother. My father would always come into the kitchen if I was eating and tell me not to eat. He would yell at me. My mother, on the other hand, was a closet eater. We never really saw her eating, so we couldn't understand why she was so fat. But she would sit up late at night to read and eat. I became a closet eater, too, because that's the way I was able to get away with it without being yelled at. So my mother and I had a lot of close ties which frustrated me because I didn't really respect who she was."

When Jody was around 15 her relationship with her mother broke down in earnest. By then Jody and the rest of the family had known for about two years of Dan's affair. "I couldn't tolerate my mother and her relationship with Dad at that point." Although Jennifer was angry, she was basically accepting of her husband's infidelity. "I was 13 when I knew that he was having an affair and it wasn't until I was 23 that he actually divorced my mother and married the woman he was having an affair with. My parents fought a lot during those years, but they were fighting over you-don't-love-me-anymore type things. My mother would insist that we not hate my father, but there was such anger there and she didn't know what to do and she didn't have the strength to walk away."

When Jody was about 16, her parents positioned her as their mediator. "All of a sudden, I was being pitted between them. What I got out of it was that my mother had no self-esteem and she needed to find herself. So I suggested in the summer of my senior year in high school that they separate so that my mother could get herself together. They took my advice. Then I went away to college, and my father came back because he figured that my mother couldn't take care of herself. Then my father's health started declining and he just said, 'I need to divorce; your mother's going to kill me.' Because my mother had such anger, she would not confront what was happening head-on. It would always come out sideways, because she didn't know how to defend herself, she didn't know how to stand up for herself. She didn't know who she was. She was Mrs. So-and-So. She was his wife. She was his secretary. She was wrapped up in him. For example, if he didn't come home at night, we would barely get fed. We would get hot dogs or something like that because she wouldn't make a big meal for us if he wasn't going to benefit."

Jennifer's and Dan's relationship took a number of twists and turns over the course of the marriage. Jennifer's anger toward her husband was one of the few constants, however. "My mother was thinner when they married, but as time went on, she got angrier and angrier, and heavier and heavier. My father had a nervous breakdown when he was 32 after a long depressive episode. It was the year I was born. He was in therapy for seven years, and from the way my mother tells it, she was the one who pumped him up and gave him his ego, his strength, and then he just went wild. She made a monster out of him, she used to say. I don't believe that she had that much power. I think she basically lost herself in the relationship. And once she lost herself she wasn't like a woman; she was like a child. In fact, my father always called her his fourth child. So he didn't have any respect for her."

Jody sees her mother as a woman who "just wanted to be loved and liked." But, she admits, "It's very hard to deal with my mother because she does not say what her feelings are, or when she does, what comes out is very warped. She doesn't confront the person she's angry with. Instead, she'll say, 'I can't hurt them.' She's more concerned for somebody else's feelings than she is for her own, so I think she's ineffective because she doesn't bring herself to a relationship."

One consequence of Jennifer's ineffectiveness was that she did not defend her daughters against their father's critical behavior. "Basically my father would tell my mother to shut up. He would say, 'You can't say anything.' So my mother was very much in the background. She was very nonverbal. She couldn't get a foothold in the family. She just had to sit by. And what I would do is sit with her to give her advice as a 15-year-old. I would say, 'This is what you should be doing, Mom.' And she would pour her problems out to me, and I felt like they had put me in an adult role of mediator when I wanted to be a child." Jody, then, became angry at her mother's reliance on her to take over the parental role.

"I had a lot of problems with her because I was her alter ego. I was the one giving her advice. I was the one telling her how to be—how to be a wife, how to be a mother. Basically, I was telling her how to be herself. I was just trying to get her to focus in on who she was and what she needed. But as far as my own needs from my mother went, I didn't get any help and that made me very angry. Yet, I didn't know how angry I was until I was older and had the wisdom of hindsight. As an adolescent, I was just trying to keep it together for them, my parents. I was just trying to counsel my mother on how to get herself together. But she was too angry at my father to even care about herself. So she was ineffective because we did not embrace her as a mother, and she did not embrace the mother image either. She would rather be off playing tennis. She'd say, 'If I had it to do over again, I wouldn't have kids.' "

Jody's leadership role in the family led to a classic symptom of a child of an ineffective parent: her own self-esteem began to diminish. "I, myself, became very lost. Both of my parents saw me as a goody-two-shoes who could take care of myself. So I felt within the family, whenever we got together as a whole, that I disappeared. I was invisible because I could take care of myself; I didn't need anything from anybody. I felt very left out. I felt like nobody really cared and nobody could understand me. If problems did come up and I went to my mother, she would just give me a sweeping, 'Well, that's the way kids are,' which didn't help me with who I was. So I never really got a validity of feeling. Neither one of my parents ever conveyed to me, 'Your feelings are valid and who you are is valid and what you feel is valid.' "

As an adult, Jody has had to struggle to establish her own sense of self—the very thing she tried so hard to help her mother attain. "In my early twenties, I got involved in very manipulative relationships, kind of like my mother and my father, where the men were just emotionally abusing me and I was taking it. One boyfriend would say things like, 'If it wasn't for me, you wouldn't be here.' I got involved in this destructive relationship with a man who was telling me who I was and defining me. I couldn't go out and buy a piece of clothing without his approval—that's how bad I was getting. But on some level I felt I had to live out my mother's relationship with my father in order for me to know what it was and to get past it, because as much as I said I would never get involved with somebody like my father, I did. So my self-esteem from 23 to 28 was just shot.

"The difference, though, between me and my mother was that I got out of this relationship by choice. Then I swore to myself that I would never get involved in an emotionally abusive relationship again. By then, I realized that it wasn't enough to simply know who you are, but that I had to act on who I was. So now I'm honest. If people try to tell me who I am, I tell them who I am. I don't stand for people trying to define me."

In terms of her relationship with her mother, Jody is still suffering feelings of invalidation, however. She feels that she is still being ignored, that her mother is favoring Elaine. "My mother's and Kim's perception of me is that I'm a clone of Elaine, and I get very angry at that because I have my own set of feelings and thoughts. But, again, it's like I'm the invisible woman. Whenever we get together I always feel like I'm left out. When my mother talks to me about coming to Los Angeles for a visit she says, 'Yes, I want to come out and I want to see you girls and I want to see Elaine's office and Elaine's house,' and I feel, 'What about me? What do you want to see about me?' Although I don't say it to her, because it's too hard for me, it just hurts. I always feel like she doesn't really care about me. She's just so concerned right now in this part of her life to get Elaine's love for some reason."

Jody believes her mother's courting of Elaine is related to the fact that Jennifer was cut off from her oldest daughter most of her life by Dan. "My father told her to stay out. Basically, he said that she couldn't have a relationship with Elaine. I think she feels very guilty about that and maybe some anger too for having fed into it and said, 'Okay, Elaine is your kid. You can have Elaine.' And then when they divorced, my mother felt, 'Oh, God, I don't have anybody.' She was very surprised when her kids were supportive of her, and she was surprised about Elaine being there for her, in particular. Now it just seems to be her life's mission to get Elaine's love."

Jody also believes that Jennifer is trying to make up to all of her daughters for her overall ineffectiveness as a parent but is going about it in the wrong way. Jody depicts her mother's behavior as being "caught up in the caricature of what a mother should be. She spent her married life caught up in what she felt a wife should be. Now she's acting out for us. A mother should worry, so she worries about me because I'm single and I'm 32. She's worried about what happens when she dies—will we have enough money or whatever. And it's like coming out of left field for me, because she never really worried about us as kids. It feels like a carica-ture. It feels like 'the shoulds'—I should be a mother because now I'm not a wife.' "

As a result, Jody says that her and her sisters' relationship with their mother lacks balance and reciprocity. "We have always been able to tell our mother how we feel about her, tell her how she made us feel, but she could never really tell us how we made her feel. She's afraid that if she tells us the truth she won't have a relationship with us. Her fear is proba-bly the fear of rejection."

So even though Jennifer is scrambling these days to establish some sort of relationship with her children, she's repeating the same co-dependent patterns that her plagued primary relationships for years. "She's still dealing with us as she has always dealt with everybody. If, for example, she came to Elaine and me and said, 'I'm really upset. I don't want to stay in a hotel when I come to visit over the holidays,' then we would talk about our reasons for suggesting that she not stay with us. Instead, she's chosen to say to Elaine—she hasn't discussed this with me— 'I know who you are, Elaine, and I know that I can't stay with you because of who you are and so if I want to see you, I'm going to have to do it on your terms.'

"That's very understanding, but it puts her in the position of always being the one to make amends. She's always the one to compromise. She's always the one to put her thoughts and feelings and needs last. But I say that's the way my mother wants to be treated, so that's the way she is treated. Kim is outraged at Elaine and me because we feed into that. But I say that until my mother is willing to assert herself, that's the way I'm going to treat her, because I have my needs too. I understand that is what my father did to her, but that's what my mother feels love is—meeting somebody else's needs at your own expense."

Postscript

A classically ineffective parent, Jennifer focused virtually all of her attention, energy, and love on her husband, a man who did not care for her. During their 30-year marriage, Jennifer became a doormat to prove her love to Dan. She placed his perceived needs above her children, her mother, her friends. She loved him obsessively. Indeed, she was a love addict, which subsequently proved to be every bit as damaging to her life and the lives of her children as more well-recognized addictions, such as workaholism or alcoholism.

Elaine, Kim, and Jody were abandoned by their mother in a variety of ways. Elaine was Dan's favorite child, so he dominated his daughter's time and literally banned Jennifer from having anything much to do with her. In keeping with her belief that she should do whatever it took to make Dan happy, Jennifer simply stood on the sidelines and refused to insist that she be allowed to take part in her daughter's upbringing. To this day, Elaine is still treated as the family hero and is courted by Jennifer for approval. Jody, the youngest daughter, who is studying to become a family counselor, believes that her mother places such importance on winning Elaine's love and respect because of guilt over how she ignored Elaine for so many years.

Jennifer abandoned Kim and Jody by reversing roles with them. As teenagers, both daughters were required to give Jennifer advice to help her sort out her life, especially when her unloving husband engaged in a 10-year affair with a much younger woman.

Typical of children of ineffective parents, all three daughters have displayed co-dependent symptoms that are directly related to their ineffective upbringing. All have experienced varying degrees of anger at their mother. Elaine has suffered over the years with periods of inexplicable fear and anxiety. At such times she believes that there is no safe place for her, that she doesn't really have a home, that there is no one for her to lean on. It is no coincidence, then, that she often repeats, "My mother was never there for me." She adds, "My relationship with her is very difficult now because, for me at least, it's sort of too late for her to be a mother. I don't need a mother anymore."

Kim responded to the emotional weight and responsibility her mother placed on her shoulders by becoming the scapegoat, the family rebel. During her adolescence, she used drugs and acted out sexually. As she grew older, she began to repress a great deal of her anger and has subsequently suffered from bouts of depression. Jody's anger revealed itself in the pattern she followed in her relationships with men during most of her twenties: she chose emotionally abusive boyfriends who required her to behave like a doormat, just as her mother behaved with her father.

Jennifer as well has suffered in that she has never regained the respect of her daughters and she herself has grown very little over the years. Just as her husband often referred to her as his fourth child, Jennifer's offspring view her as childlike, an adult who is simply not in touch with her own potential.

As with any family, Jennifer and her daughters are recovering at their own individual paces. From all reports, Jennifer is happier now than she has ever been, but her pattern of ineffectiveness hasn't changed much. Instead, she has replaced Dan with Elaine in her lifelong attempt to woo the unwinnable. Jennifer wants Elaine to love her, to let her be the mother she failed to be many years ago. Thus far, Elaine has been unwilling to comply. Jennifer, then, is repeating her doormat pattern by trying to pull from her daughter what Elaine does not want to give.

Elaine has received therapy over the years and in general is doing well. It's been a while since one of her periods of "free-floating anxiety." Her marriage of 17 years is thriving. She is, however, uncomfortable with the hero role her mother and other family members have assigned her. Indeed, she pays a price for the presumed accolade: She is revered but at times resented by the very people who have placed her on the pedestal.

Kim, a part-time accountant and part-time weaver, is beginning to explore her artistic side, something she has wanted to do for years. She's also happily married, although she admits that she still has times when she is very depressed and unhappy. Jody's recovery program appears to be on solid ground as demonstrated by her fairly clear understanding of herself and her history and of what she needs to do to avoid self-destructive, co-dependent patterns of behavior. She still feels insecure and "invisible," though, when her mother indicates she's more interested in Elaine than in Jody's accomplishments.

The picture that emerges of Jennifer is one of an ineffective parent who has unwittingly painted herself into a corner through her co-dependent need to reduce herself in order to put someone else in charge of her life's circumstances. As an outsider, though, it was hard for me to feel anything but compassion for Jennifer's basic emotional ineptness and her aloneness at this stage of her life. It's that feeling of compassion that led me to the important lesson I learned from this chapter: the lesson of forgiveness.

There is no doubt that Jennifer's ineffectiveness caused her three daughters a great deal of pain, but she too has suffered by living a love-addicted life full of regrets and recriminations. It's also true that my father's compulsive gambling caused him to fail to accept his responsibilities as a parent. Yet, recounting and rethinking my own past with an ineffective parent has caused me to view my father in a somewhat different light: I simply don't believe that my father wanted to hurt us children, so I am left to conclude that he must have behaved the way he did because he lost control of his own life, particularly as he became an addicted gambler.

I have developed compassion for my father by noting how his co-dependent behavior paralleled Jennifer's. Her fundamental unhappiness caused me to think about what my father must have felt on any given day of his life. Listening to Jennifer's testimony helped me to understand how powerless ineffective parents believe themselves to be. My process of forgiveness began in earnest when I finally realized that the pain of my own suffering had blinded me from seeing that my father paid an even higher price than I for his mistakes.

To start to forgive your mother or father's ineffectiveness, begin by making a list of at least five of your parents' worst character traits that caused you the most grief during your childhood and perhaps continue to hurt you now. Then create a column labeled "Feelings" to the right of your list to identify emotions generally associated with such traits displayed by your parents. For example, if you have a parent who lies a lot, list that as a trait; and then under the "Feelings" column you would probably write "fear and insecurity."

If, at times, you or your spouse are ineffective parents, work through this exercise by honestly listing those co-dependent behaviors that make you the most uncomfortable. Then think about what you are feeling when you act in this manner.

Whether you are scrutinizing your parents or yourself, what you will develop is a chart that demonstrates just how human we all are.

PART 3

RECOVERY–TAKING ACTION, BREAKING PATTERNS

By now you know which co-dependent parenting model or models you have been practicing for years, and you may feel acutely guilty about how your behavior has affected your child. Part Three provides you with the tools to transcend your pain, overcome your guilt, and pursue your recovery in earnest.

Chapter 8 explains the distinctions between taking refuge in blame, being paralyzed by guilt, and embracing responsibility. Chapter 9 introduces you to a concept of recovery that may be new to you: Recovery is not a finite activity. Instead, it's a process that will engage you for the rest of your life.

Chapter 9's Four-Phase Healing Program asks that you work through a number of exercises designed to help you make peace with your parents; make peace with yourself; make peace with your child; and become a validating parent.

CHAPTER 8

COPING WITH AWARENESS

I discovered that I was a co-dependent while doing research for another book, *Parents Who Help Their Children Overcome Drugs*. The revelation sent me into a tailspin that lasted several months. Of course I knew that I was not perfect, that I had developed some unhealthy behavioral patterns along the way. And, to some degree, my recovery process had already begun for some readily recognizable habits that I wanted to change, such as my propensity to unjustly criticize others as well as myself. But to learn that I fit the profile of an addictive personality, someone who needed to be needed, clashed with my image of myself.

Most of my adult life had been spent playing the role of the family hero; I was the overachiever. In recent years, as it was revealed that my sister had become addicted to crack cocaine, I took my hero's role even more seriously. My superwoman act was expanded to include not only professional accomplishments but physical achievements as well. Maintaining my good health took on a new meaning for me. In addition to my long-time practice of vegetarianism, I hired a personal body trainer and began heavy weight lifting. I spent my weekends running up and down the bleachers at the local high school to strengthen my legs. So to learn that my workaholism and need to control my sister's and son's lives demonstrated co-dependency—a type of addiction in its own right—came as quite a shock and literally caused me to go into hiding for a few months.

Basically, what I had to come to grips with was that my self-image had been irrevocably pierced. And that hurt. It was hard to face the fact that I was not as emotionally healthy as I once believed. It was more difficult to acknowledge that my unhealthiness had had an adverse impact on others, especially people whom I dearly loved, such as my sister and son. So I felt pain because of my bruised self-image, overwhelming guilt, and because I was masking fear. I did not want my son to blame me for all of his problems as an adult. This was a particularly sticky point since I had sworn to myself that I would never make the same mistakes in parenting that my mother had made. It was hard for me to accept that I had replicated some of my mother's behavior in raising my son.

Not surprisingly, many months passed before I told my adult child what I had learned about myself: that I was a co-dependent, that I had orchestrated his emotional subjugation in order to feel good about myself. My procrastination, it turns out, was unwarranted; my worst visions of how my son would respond did not come to pass. He did not attack me. He questioned me and we talked, and we continue to talk. In fact, sharing my shortcomings with him became the basis for his feeling comfortable enough to share his human frailties with me. Our relationship has been inexorably altered for the better by my acknowledgments.

By now you have read about the five primary co-dependent parenting models in Part Two of this book and have no doubt recognized your own symptoms in one or more of these descriptions. You are probably grappling with some of the same feelings I initially experienced: shock, disillusionment, guilt, and the fear of being blamed by your child or others for your mistakes. Such feelings are to be expected. Indeed, these feelings constitute the beginning of your recovery process. No matter how bad you may feel at this moment, you have broken through your denial and are acknowledging your history of co-dependent parenting, which is the first step toward learning how to transcend your human imperfections. Coping with your newfound awareness, however, is tough. The feelings that are typically stirred up when a parent uncovers his co-dependency are very uncomfortable. Coping gets easier, though, when you understand more about the feelings to which you are probably clinging. And significant rewards await the parents and families who can move beyond these feelings.

DROPPING BLAME AND GUILT, EMBRACING RESPONSIBILITY

Blame and guilt are directly related to the concept of punishment. Generally, when these feelings arise between parent and child they are associated with a belief that the love of one for the other is in question. For example, when a parent is fearful of accepting a heavy burden of blame for her child's behavioral problems, that parent is wary that she will be punished by her offspring for having made mistakes during the child's upbringing. The anticipated punishment is that the child will withdraw his love from the parent, although such fears are rarely spoken.

That was my underlying though unacknowledged fear when I realized that I was a co-dependent parent. So I postponed sharing that realization with my adult son.

When you carry around a lot of guilt, on the other hand, you are punishing yourself for not living up to your own value system. You feel pain because you believe you have broken at least three of your own moral codes: (1) that parents should be perfect; (2) that being perfect means taking excellent care of your child; and (3) that a demonstration of excellence is the best representation of a parent's love. Accepting some of the blame for the development of my son's co-dependency caused me to feel guilty. I felt like a bad mother because to falter was to fail, according to my standards. Underneath it all, I felt like a mother who must not have really loved her son. I believed that others might question my love for my son since I had allowed him to be harmed by my co-dependent imperfections. Consequently, I punished myself by clinging to anguish and self-pity. I chastised myself. I became depressed. I took no positive action to help myself or my son during this period. Between fearing blame and feeling guilt, I became immobilized. For a while, I could not cope with the awareness of my co-dependent parenting.

Blame and guilt, then, are feelings that disempower. As parents we are disempowered when we allow our fears and self-indictments to stop us from attempting to change our behavior. We prevent ourselves from bettering our own lives and those of our family when we are so frightened by the specter of blame and guilt that we deny our co-dependency in favor of upholding an informal status quo that implies we always know best. Denial works against us as parents because it reflects a self-serving moral code that encourages us to hide behind a shield of imagined perfection, which at some point becomes self-defeating. Eventually we are imprisoned by what is meant to protect us. In other words, we can't change co-dependent behavior that we refuse to acknowledge. Thus, we put ourselves in the position of not being able to do the best for ourselves and for our children.

I broke my pattern of retreat when I discovered that there was another legitimate way of looking at my situation. Yes, I had made mistakes. Yes, I was a co-dependent parent, and there was no denying that my co-dependency had at times hurt my child. But I did not have to continue to behave in this matter and I did not have to fear my son or myself. I learned that *I* could decide what triggers my guilt response by changing some of the moral codes that underlie my value system. For example, I discarded my belief that parents should be perfect and replaced it with a more real-istic rule: Healthy parents strive to be honest, not perfect.

I also learned that I could trade feelings of blame for those associated with accepting responsibility. Accepting responsibility allowed me to ac-knowledge my mistakes, feel some measure of grief, and then move for-ward with strength and the resolve to do better. Once I gave up my feel-ings of blame and guilt, I felt in control of myself and my ability to take action. Yet my new response did not involve the denial of my history or my feelings. Instead, when I embraced responsibility I embraced self-acceptance—a concept that recognizes the possibility that sometimes we make mistakes.

CHALLENGING THE STATUS QUO

Admittedly, it's not easy to break deeply entrenched patterns of co-dependent behavior, particularly since to do so means we as parents need to find ways to see ourselves in a different light, to recognize our symp-toms perhaps for the first time. Choosing to recover requires that we challenge the status quo at some point. The existing state of affairs in most households reflects a complex dynamic that is typically uncon-scious and virtually always long-standing, as discussed in previous chap-ters. Co-dependent symptoms are routinely and unwittingly passed along from one generation to another. The symptoms often are subtle and con-nected in fundamental ways to our self-esteem, self-image, and relation-ship with our own parents (whether they are alive or dead). So there is much to untangle and much to confront. To that end, the exercises at the ends of Chapters 3 through 7 have helped you begin to unravel what has gone on in your life, to help you see more clearly what needs to be changed and why.

Parents as Victims of Victims

At the end of Chapter 3, The Demanding Parent, you were asked to identify at least three areas of struggle you had with your parents and then examine the way you deal with your own children around these very same issues. Were you surprised to discover that you are doing some of the same things to your children that your parents did to you? By becom-ing aware of your parents' co-dependent traits, did you also notice your own and those of your child?

One of the primary areas of conflict I had with my mother concerned her demanding demeanor, which was based upon her unyielding belief that she was always right and I was always wrong. So I had strong feelings about never becoming as rigid as she has been. Yet when I asked my son many years later what he thought I needed to work on to better our relationship, he said, "Mom, you always have to be right, and that's hard to handle." In turn, I have received telephone calls from my son's girlfriends over the years complaining about *his* need to be right all of the time.

The purpose of Chapter 3's exercise was to help you see that just as you were a victim of your parents' co-dependency, your child will be a victim of the family's co-dependent legacy—unless you attempt to break the cycle by first becoming aware and then acting on that awareness. This exercise can also help to put in a different perspective the inclination many of us have to unforgivingly blame our parents for our troubles. It does so by setting up a useful juxtaposition—aligning your good intentions next to those of your parents. You know that as a parent you have wanted to do the best for your child. Even so, you made mistakes in raising your offspring because of your own unconscious co-dependency handed down to you by your parents. Given that this is so in your case, isn't there a strong possibility that the same was true of your own parents? Does it make sense to blame a victim? In Chapter 9, you will find exercises to help you pass along to your child what you are learning about yourself. By so doing, your son or daughter can begin to develop a new and more healthy awareness about you just as you are developing greater awareness in regard to your own parents.

The Importance of Watching Our P's and Q's

Chapter 4's exercise, which dealt with the consequences of critical parenting, asked you to list at least five pivotal incidents from your childhood that had a significant impact on you. You were then requested to compose a similar list of incidents between you and your offspring that you believe your child might consider important. Was it more difficult for you to determine crucial moments in your relationship with your child than it was to list troublesome exchanges that took place between your parents and yourself? Did you find yourself at a loss to come up with five such incidents in your child's life?

At first, it was difficult for me to do so because I was in denial. But then I remembered a conversation I had with my then-13-year-old son some years ago, during which he spent several hours citing incident after incident of poor parenting choices I had made. The point of Chapter 4's exercise, then, is to help you understand the level of influence we as parents have on our children. Virtually everything we say and do—even comments and actions that we deem inconsequential—play some role in our children's development.

This exercise also demonstrates the value of trying to see yourself through your child's eyes. Can you honestly say that your child's view of your co-dependent character as demonstrated by your behavior matches your self-image? Does it match the image of the person you always thought you were or want to be? If it does not—which is the finding I had to face—you will have an opportunity in Chapter 9 to work through some additional exercises that will help you and your child heal old wounds as well as reconstruct your relationship.

Understanding the Love-Fear Connection

In Chapter 5, which examined what it meant to be an overprotective parent, the end-of-chapter exercise consisted of listing at least five activities you performed, against your better judgment, to please your child. In addition, you were asked to write in detail about what motivated you to put the gaining of your son's or daughter's approval above all other considerations. At first glance, do your reasons for your behavior appear noble and selfless? Upon taking a closer look, however, is there a common thread to be found in your justifications: the underlying fear of losing your child's love? If, after honest examination, that is the case, do you have any idea as to why you believe your child's love is so tenuous?

Mary, the mother of the family profile in Chapter 5, painfully admits that she still caters to and covers for her 22-year-old son because she fears she might otherwise lose his love. For example, this overprotective mother assumed the responsibility of making a number of telephone calls to track down her son when he did not show up for his scheduled interview for this book. She did everything within her power to try to make up for her son's irresponsibility.

This exercise was designed to help you move your overprotective behavior out of the closet to see it for what it is: a way of bartering for your child's love in order to quell your own fears of inadequacy. If you are not an overprotective parent but are laboring with symptoms of other co-dependent parenting models, you can also benefit from this exercise because it will permit you to gain some insight into what really motivates your behavior. In Chapter 9 you will find exercises that will help you enhance your self-esteem, develop healthy ways to express how much you care for your child, and build your confidence that your child will love you for what you are.

Looking Out for Number One–The Downside

The exercise at the end of Chapter 6 involved listing the major activities in your life according to how much time you devote to each. You were asked to prioritize your list by putting the activities at the top that take up the most time and then indicating next to each activity who really benefits from it. Did your children rank at the top of the list as primary benefactors of the disengaging behavior that keeps you preoccupied, or did you?

As with overprotective parents, it's easy for a disengaging parent–one who is a workaholic, for instance–to insist that her co-dependent behavior is strictly for the purpose of providing the best in material objects for her child. If, after honestly assessing your motivations, you still believe that you do what you do for your child, ask yourself whether your child has ever suggested that he would like more of your time and less of your money. If so, stop again and ask yourself why you are working so hard.

When I was finally willing to get tough with myself in answering this question, I was surprised to find out that my workaholism had very little to do with my son's betterment. Instead, I discovered that I was unconsciously looking out for number one by becoming a superachiever in my attempts to gain my parents' approval. In truth, for a long time I was so self-absorbed that I paid virtually no attention to the fact that my son was not being well nurtured.

Again, the purpose of this exercise is to help you see your co-dependent behavior more clearly so that you are motivated to change rather than to hide behind a false image of yourself. Exercises in Chapter 9 will help you resolve the conflicts you have with your own parents so that you don't feel compelled to live a life that requires you to pedal as fast as you can to win your own parents' love.

To Err Is Human

At the end of Chapter 7 you were requested to list at least five traits of your parents that were most difficult to deal with. The next part of the exercise asked you to identify the common emotions associated with the behaviors your parents regularly displayed. If you had determined that you were also an ineffective parent, you were asked to work through this exercise for yourself as well. Were you surprised by what you found out about your parents and yourself?

I already knew my father had been an insecure personality based upon the way he avoided emotional confrontation with my mother and others. But working through this exercise helped me to see something else—that my father lived much of his life as a desperate man. As I thought about the times when he would take me to the racetrack and then con me out of a substantial portion of my winnings—or borrow large sums of money and then with a plaintive voice ask me not to tell my mother—for the first time I could visualize the kind of fear and desperation he must have tolerated for years. That one insight helped to dissipate a lot of my anger toward him for being so ineffective and not really helping to raise me.

What I hoped to accomplish with the exercises in Chapter 7 was to help you see your parents and yourself in more compassionate terms. None of us is perfect. We are all prone to making egregious errors at times simply because we are human. To see that your parents are as human as the next person is to see that you too are subject to human frailties in your efforts to raise a healthy and prosperous child. You will find exercises in Chapter 9 that prepare you to forgive not only your parents for the mistakes they made with you but also yourself for the mistakes you have made with your offspring. Other exercises will show you how to help your child forgive you for your history of co-dependent parenting.

TRADING THE OLD IMAGE FOR THE NEW

Basically, all of the exercises in this book are designed to help you discover the multi-dimensionality of your parents, yourself, and your children. That is to say, they are designed to help you see yourself and your family members more clearly and to act on what you see. In the relationship between the co-dependent parent and child, it's particularly important we make sure that our children see us as we really are, because co-dependent parenting of any kind has as its tenet the need to hide feelings, and thereby foment distrust, as described in Chapter 2 (see the section on Dysfunctional Families and the Three 'Don'ts'). Depending on the nature of the parent-child dynamic, there is also a tendency for many mothers and fathers to succumb to the mythic hero syndrome—or its opposite, the wicked witch or Darth Vader syndrome, depending on gender. All are troublesome images.

Parents who abide by the mythic hero syndrome either set themselves on a pedestal or allow their children to place them on a pedestal so that they are deemed incapable of doing wrong. Critical, demanding, and overprotective parents to greater or lesser degrees fall into this category. These parents have a common need to control their children by virtue of their rightness and righteousness; this need is displayed overtly by critical and demanding parents, and covertly by overprotective parents. Since no one can be right all the time, their perch on the pedestal is stressful and precarious, for they must monitor their every action in an ongoing attempt to maintain the facade. Paradoxically, these parents tend to produce rebellious or scapegoat children who at some point become their parents' worst nightmare, because rebel children are looking for ways to knock these parents off of their throne. By accepting the mythic hero role, such parents also pay a price because they believe they are loved by their children for what they are not, rather than for what they are. So, in truth, there is not much joy to be experienced from the admiration they receive from their offspring.

On the other hand, mothers and fathers whose children expect little or nothing from them—as is often the case in the relationship between disengaging and ineffective parents and their offspring—the wicked witch or Darth Vader syndrome kicks in. In this instance, the child perceives the parent as being unlikely to do what is right or appropriate. Consequently, these parents "get away" with nonparenting since their children have few expectations. However, they too pay a high price. The dark image of one-dimensionality imprisons such parents as much as the saintliness of the mythic hero syndrome cuts off many healthy behavioral options. Their children will tend to discount the positive qualities of parents who fall into the wicked witch or Darth Varder syndrome, so that eventually it doesn't pay for these parents to try to upgrade their behavior.

If a bottom line can be drawn from these observations, it's that ultimately the good health and well-being of the co-dependent parent and his family cannot be achieved until that parent is ready to trade his old image for that of the new parent in recovery.

CHAPTER 9

FREEING YOURSELF, FREEING YOUR CHILD

As a disengaging parent, I hid behind a self-serving definition of freedom. From my co-dependent point of view, being free meant that I had the right to become a workaholic superachiever, even if doing so left me little time to nurture my son. In retrospect, my goal of professional freedom was a red herring I used unconsciously to sidestep involvement in my child's emotional development. Given my co-dependent upbringing, it was much easier to pursue career accomplishments than to connect emotionally with my son. Of course, by ignoring his needs, I was denying my own feelings as well. Ironically, the freedom of action I cherished ultimately circumscribed my life because of what I did *not* allow myself to do or feel.

I realize now that freedom for me is very much tied to my willingness to overcome a legacy of co-dependent parenting. As long as I hang on to my fear of emotional attachment, I will inevitably display symptoms and make choices that ensure that I raise an unhealthy child and remain an unhealthy parent. Deciding to recover, then, is the same as deciding to be truly free, because you are creating for yourself and your offspring more behavioral options than ever before. And there is an added bonus: Choosing to give up your co-dependent parenting will allow you and your child to know your real selves for the first time.

THE NATURE OF RECOVERY

Becoming acquainted with your real self, which will empower you to support a healthy family dynamic, is not as clearcut a task as it might seem. Recovering from lifelong habits of co-dependency is a complex effort. Much of the real self is hidden, often unconsciously, in a co-dependent personality. Psychoanalyst Alice Miller explains this phenomenon in her book *The Drama of the Gifted Child: The Search for the True*

Self. She labels the pre-recovery persona the "as-if personality." Miller describes the as-if personality as an adult who has learned from an early age to reveal, through the way he behaves, only what will please his parents. With time, the as-if personality "fuses so completely with what he reveals that...one could scarcely have guessed how much more there is to him, behind this 'masked view of himself.' He cannot develop and differentiate his 'true self,' because he is unable to live it."

Overcoming symptoms of co-dependent parenting, then, means learning how to reveal and live with your real self, while encouraging the same in your child. When I first glimpsed what was to be gained from my attempts to recover, I was disappointed. Viewing the world through co-dependent eyes, I anticipated that the pot of gold at the end of the rainbow would be my conversion from a disengaging mother to Supermom, the perfect parent. Grappling with so many painful emotions in order to learn how to be my unencumbered self hardly seemed worth the effort, since I couldn't guarantee the quality of the final product—my real self. I also wanted quick results. I believed that it should be possible to pinpoint a day, a moment, when I would suddenly change into an incredibly healthy person. My underlying wish, of course, was to limit the amount of time spent confronting feelings I had denied for so long, to minimize the effort to break what felt at times like intractable patterns of co-dependent behavior. Basically, I wanted a quick, easy, and painless formula for recovery.

Since then, I have discovered that it is common to have unrealistic expectations about the nature of recovery. Given what is involved in the recovery process, it's not surprising that as parents we want to race through, to consider ourselves healthy parents as soon as possible. Recovery, however, is a *process*, one that will engage us for the rest of our lives. The good news is: Our lifetime commitment to recovery is a commitment for which we and our children will be rewarded throughout.

Recovery is not a static state. In other words, we are healthy parents when we actively work at becoming healthy parents, when we understand that getting to know our real self (and the real selves of our family members) is an ever-evolving goal that provides continual rewards.

A FOUR-PHASE HEALING PROGRAM

The remaining pages of this chapter are devoted to describing a four-phase healing program that will help you: (1) Make peace with your parents; (2) make peace with yourself; (3) make peace with your child; and (4) become a validating parent. Exercises accompany each phase of this prescription for healing a legacy of co-dependent parenting. All of the concepts and exercises are interconnected and thus cut across all four phases and build on each other. Certain exercises will ask that you work through specific activities; other exercises will assist you in expanding your awareness. In general, the exercises will help you to acknowledge and then cope with long-suppressed feelings, break unhealthy behavioral patterns passed on to you by your parents, and start building a better relationship with your child.

This four-phase healing program recognizes the fact that co-dependent symptoms can only survive where there are at least two persons consciously or unconsciously playing an unhealthy game that creates and perpetuates feelings of low self-esteem for all involved. So, it is not possible to free yourself from co-dependent symptoms without also freeing your child from such patterns of behavior.

The first two phases *prepare* you for freeing your child by helping you to break the co-dependent habits you have displayed over the years. You will also be shown how to sort out your relationship with your own parents, from whom you acquired your co-dependent traits. Phases Three and Four are designed to help you *complete* a process that will lead you to your goal—freeing your child—and, while so doing, help you to free yourself from your history of co-dependency. You will be shown how to reach out to involve your son or daughter in your recovery process. In addition, Phase Four provides guidelines for establishing new patterns of behavior that reflect what it means to be a validating parent, a person who knows how to help his or her child grow up to become a healthy adult.

You will need to repeat or review periodically the exercises that comprise the four-phase healing process. Do not be surprised if each time you work through the exercises you uncover new information about yourself, your parents, and your child. You are embarking upon an evolutionary process, and each new insight is evidence that you and your family are growing and recovering.

PHASE ONE: MAKING PEACE WITH YOUR PARENTS

One of the hardest things for me to do was to forgive my parents for the type of upbringing I experienced. Even after I recognized how difficult it was to be a parent—having made more than one mistake in raising my own son—I could barely muster any compassion for my parents' misguided though often well-intentioned errors in judgment and deed. My way of dealing with my parents was to harbor feelings of resentment that in turn provoked guilt.

Finally, after years of struggling with my own recovery process and becoming frustrated with my inability to make the gains that I hoped for, I figured out what was impeding my progress: I did not see my parents as authentically multi-dimensional people who could be expected to stumble like anyone else. So I retreated emotionally from my mother and father and therefore could feel no compassion for them. Since I could not feel compassion, I could not forgive them their mistakes.

Phase One takes you through a series of exercises that will help you acknowledge your parents' multi-dimensionality as well as help you get in touch with your anger, pain, and guilt provoked by their history of imperfection. The intent is to assist you in developing genuine compassion for your parents. Moreover, there is an additional payoff: When you can begin to feel compassion for your parents, forgiveness is possible. I found out the hard way, making peace with your parents is an important factor in your ability to make peace with yourself.

Acknowledging Your Parents' Co-Dependency

It's common for children, even adult children, to avoid acknowledging their parents' co-dependency. The primary reason is that most of us are consciously or unconsciously afraid of losing our parents' approval, which we equate with losing their love. We demonstrate our fear in numerous ways. Because of the particular family dynamic that existed in my household, for example, it was easy for me to note all of my mother's shortcomings and difficult to acknowledge any flaws in my father's character. Mother's authoritarian behavior caused her to be cast as the family villain. By contrast, Father (a disengaging parent) avoided responsibility for our upbringing and discipline, and used his passive-aggressive personality to his advantage. He became an ally for us kids—a covert ally, since his support of us was almost always kept secret from Mother. We saw him as our friend—sometimes our only friend. Given this history, it's not surprising that I managed to overlook my father's co-dependent symptoms until many years after his death.

Sometimes we don't see our parents clearly because we prefer to overlook the flaws, as in my relationship with my father. Sometimes we really don't see what is obvious to others because we have idealized our parents. Our parents may have trained us to view them as mythic heroes and so have tied our identity and self-esteem to their continued tenure on a pedestal. In protecting our parents' image, we're protecting our own.

Sometimes we don't recognize our parents' co-dependency because such behavior is all we have ever known; the co-dependent environment is our norm. There are moments when I still fall into that trap, when I describe unsettling incidents from my childhood as if they were unremarkable. For example, as punishment my mother routinely isolated me from contact with my friends and the outside world for periods averaging eight to nine months at a time. This meant I had to come straight home from school and remain there until the next morning; I was not allowed to leave the house except to go to school. Once home, I was not permitted to accept or make telephone calls or to have visitors. After one such period, I remember crying over my renewed opportunity to gaze upon the moon—it looked so beautiful after being sequestered for close to a year. As an adult, when I related that tale to others, I gave no indication that my experience was anything but commonplace.

Whatever the reasons for not acknowledging our parents' co-dependency, we can jog our awareness by remembering a theme discussed throughout this book: If you are a co-dependent parent, you were raised by a co-dependent mother or father. Consequently, acknowledging your own co-dependency by definition reveals your parents' co-dependency.

You have already completed an exercise designed to expand your awareness of your parents, to help you view them as fallible human beings with strengths and weaknesses like anyone else. At the end of Chapter 3, you were asked to list at least three areas of conflicts between you and your parents. In addition, you were asked to determine if you were experiencing similar struggles with your own children, to see how the legacy of co-dependency gets passed along from one generation to another. The purpose of those exercises is to see yourself and your parents in a new and revealing frame of reference.

Exercises in the next section will provide you with some additional tools to help you accept your parents' multi-dimensionality. Even if you are an adult who has already taken an honest look at your upbringing, you can still gain some value from working through these exercises. No matter how much you understand about your childhood and the role your parents played in your development, there is always new insight to be gleaned because of the evolutionary nature of recovery.

Exercise: Your Parents, Yourself. Another way of gaining a new perspective on your relationship with your parents is to consider whether they can be placed in the same category in which you place yourself: an adult child of a co-dependent parent. Review the following list of common characteristics of adults who were raised by co-dependent parents, which was referred to in Chapter 2. This time, candidly examine each of the symptoms to determine whether *your parents*, rather than yourself, have ever displayed this type of behavior. To the extent that you recognize your own co-dependent behavior, your parents are also co-dependent: Co-dependency begets co-dependency.

Adult children of co-dependent parents share many of the following characteristics:

- They judge themselves mercilessly.
- They have difficulty having fun.
- They take themselves too seriously.
- They have difficulty with intimate relationships.
- They overreact to changes they cannot control.
- They constantly seek approval and affirmation.
- They lie when it would be just as easy to tell the truth.
- They are extremely loyal even when the loyalty is undeserved.
- They are either super-responsible or super-irresponsible.
- They have difficulty following a project through from beginning to end.
- They are unsure of what is normal or inappropriate behavior, and often have to guess at how to behave.
- They are impulsive; they tend to lock themselves into a course of action without giving serious consideration to alternative behaviors or possible consequences.
- They usually feel they are different from other people.

Exercise: Exposing Family Secrets. Another way to determine whether you were raised in a co-dependent household is to list all the family secrets your parents explicitly or implicitly required you to keep. Once you have made the list, ask yourself the following questions:

- What was at stake if any of these secrets had been allowed to surface among the family? Your parents' image of themselves? The family's image to outsiders?
- Did many of the secrets involve your hiding the way you really felt?

Parents who foster a domestic environment that puts pressure on their children to conceal or suppress their genuine emotions or honest thoughts are demonstrating classic symptoms of co-dependency.

Exercise: Parents—Through the Eyes of Others. Another exercise to help you obtain a clearer view of your parents is to try to see them through the eyes of other family members. If you have sisters and brothers, call them. Begin a dialogue with them about their childhood observations, about their view of your parents' behavior. Does it coincide with your own recollections? Don't be surprised if there is a difference; their experience with your parents will differ from yours because you are different people. Still, if you can see that you exhibit co-dependent symptoms but cannot identify any such flaws in your parents' character, then chances are there is some obstruction of your vision, some denial that may be overcome by shifting to another point of view.

Acknowledging Your Pain

Acknowledging your parents' co-dependency can provoke a range of painful emotions such as rage, resentment, depression, impotence, and betrayal. Often we are tempted to suppress what is an important part of ourselves because of guilt (it's uncomfortable to have negative thoughts about our parents no matter how we were treated) and because we may not know how to express our feelings if we were discouraged from doing so as children.

Getting to know our parents' real selves is bound to generate an emotional response. And feelings that are not dealt with do not go away, they only become distorted and hurt us at some later date. Feeling disapproval from my parents as a child, for example, led to my "bionic woman" syndrome as an adult, since I internalized my hurt and rejection because I did not know how to sort out what I felt.

The exercises below will help you to understand that your pain is real and valid and that it's okay to explore what you feel—even if the feeling is rage.

Exercise: Scripts as Healing Tools. If it is difficult for you to pinpoint which emotions are activated when your mother or father displays co-dependent symptoms, writing a script to re-create a typical, troublesome exchange between yourself and your parents may help you get in touch with your feelings. For example, if your mother was a critical parent, write down or tape record what she might say to you to cause you to feel wrong. Then write or record your normal response. Now, stop and try to identify the feelings that have been jarred by engaging in this exercise. If you were raised to simply feel nothing, then acknowledge the experience of nothingness and begin to examine what that must mean. Ask yourself, how might anyone be expected to react to a derogatory expression from his or her mother? Then ask yourself whether it's really true that you feel nothing.

Thirty-year-old John, a Texan whom I interviewed for this book, applied this technique to help him understand what he felt when dealing with his critical parent, his mother. John's script even included his thoughts.

> JOHN: Mom, it bothers me that you said what you said about me to my *wife* instead of me.
>
> MOM: Oh. Well, you're wrong to feel that way.
>
> JOHN: (I have all of these mixed emotions. It's so hard for me to be angry with my mother. It confuses me.)

As he began to examine this and other exchanges with his mother, he came to understand that "I can get angry with my parents and still love them."

Exercise: Keeping a Journal.   One exercise you can undertake to transcend the pain you are probably feeling from starting the process of humanizing your parents is to keep a journal. Write down what you feel. If you don't like to write, speak into a tape recorder. The advantage of translating your feelings into the written or recorded word is that you can read or play back what you have expressed and learn more each time the exercise is revisited. You get to work on you, instead of initiating a confrontation with your parents that has a hidden agenda—you may want to blame or change them, rather than to sort out yourself.

Margo, the adult daughter from the family profile in Chapter 4, used the journal technique when she discovered that her history of starting out strong in romantic relationships and ending up needy and abused was tied to a co-dependent pattern established years ago with her father. The following is an excerpt from her journal:

> In my relationships with men, I continually re-create my relationship with my father. What was my childhood relationship to my father? He was rejecting! And what is my "button" now in relationships? Rejection. And while as an adult I have the opportunity to handle rejection differently than I did as a child, I continue to deal with it pretty much as I always did. I don't express my anger. I become insecure, anxious, sullen, inwardly angry. But I am afraid to express the anger to the man because I risk the greatest rejection—abandonment.

When my father rejected me, I withdrew into myself, determined to survive without his love. But inside I felt rage and impotence at not being able to confront him either directly with my
anger or to negotiate reconciliation—*I had no power in relation
to him.* Then he died and I never got to express to him how he
made me feel. So how do I stop re-creating my past relationship
with my father? I resolve the conflict by creating a written dialogue with him to express my hurt and rage.

Margo would not let me see what she subsequently wrote, because it
included profane language. She said she threw a tantrum on paper. But
when she was through, she felt relieved, emotionally unburdened for the
first time in 42 years.

Exercise: Writing Letters   Another exercise that will help you cope with
whatever pain you may be feeling is to write your parents a letter or as
many letters as you need to express your pent-up emotions over how you
were raised. There is no need to mail what you have written, because the
point of this exercise is to assist you in getting in touch with what *you*
feel, not your parents' reaction to what you feel.

Releasing Your Guilt

Once you have allowed yourself to accept and vent your pain, you are
probably feeling some guilt. After all, we are indebted to our parents for
our very lives. We were totally dependent on them to provide the most
fundamental of needs—food, clothing, shelter, and love. Virtually all of us
harbor a hidden fear of losing our parents' love. So you may be feeling
some guilt for being angry with your parents' co-dependent behavior. For
children of any age, there is often a perceived risk associated with feeling
anything except loving gratitude toward their mother or father.

If guilt is allowed to linger, it will thwart your attempts to recover
from co-dependency, because the underlying implication of guilt is that
you are wrong to feel whatever you are feeling about your parents. As
long as you believe that you are not entitled to your feelings, you will
second-guess what generated those feelings, and you will cover up, tell
lies, and create fantasies about your childhood to try to feel okay, to try to
"protect" your parents or your image of them. Actually, you are really
trying to protect yourself.

Exercise: Create New Moral Codes   Jan, the 32-year-old sister of John
from Texas, is currently in therapy to "be able to say who I am, and be able

to cope with the fact that my parents may not approve of that." However, she asked that her real name not be used in this book for fear that her mother would be hurt if she found out what Jan really feels. Jan experiences a great deal of guilt about her real feelings: anger and resentment from "never having received unconditional love from my mother. There was always a 'but' or 'what if.' "

Jan is beginning to release her guilt by analyzing her moral codes and thus is learning a valuable lesson: When we feel guilt, it's because we have broken one of our moral codes, the belief system that underpins our values. Indeed, without a moral code, there is no guilt. Most of us, however, devote little time to thinking about these significant rules that govern our lives. Given Jan's critical upbringing, her moral codes include:

1. I should protect my mother above all else.
2. I should do whatever it takes to gain my mother's approval.
3. I should hide my "negative" feelings from my parents, particularly my mother.

To a large degree, Jan's value system devalues and at times invalidates her emotions in favor of her parents. By developing a new set of moral codes, Jan could release guilt feelings over her anger about her co-dependent upbringing. For example, she could replace the three moral codes above with:

1. My behavior reflects activity that supports and maintains my integrity and well-being.
2. I value my opinion of myself over anyone else's opinion of me.
3. I live an honest emotional life.

Once she begins to live by these new codes, when feelings of guilt arise, she can examine her new codes to see if there is some basis for her feelings of guilt. If not, she could begin to ask herself: Why am I hanging on to my guilt? What's in it for me if I continue to live by my old value system?

You, too, can develop a new set of moral codes to help you cope with guilt feelings provoked by working through earlier exercises in this chapter. Follow the same procedure described for Jan. First, examine your guilt over feeling hostility toward your parents because of their co-dependent parenting. Then assess why you believe you have violated your values. Do this by repeating as many times as necessary: "I feel guilty because..."

When I completed this sentence, I said:

1. I feel guilty because my father was so much nicer than my mother, therefore I shouldn't think anything bad about him.
2. I feel guilty because now that my mother has grown older she has mellowed and is not as difficult, so I shouldn't continue to feel rage over her past behavior.
3. I feel guilty because I shouldn't get angry with my parents or anyone else.

Translated into moral codes, these phrases would become:

1. I think kind thoughts about my father because he was so much nicer than my mother.
2. I am grateful that my mother has mellowed and displays more kindness.
3. I always feel warmth for my parents.

Your responses to the "I feel guilty because..." phrase will help determine your current moral codes. Once you have compiled your list, study it carefully. Are you surprised by your basic beliefs about life? If so, change them. You have control over your belief system, even if it is long-standing. You can alter beliefs that trigger feelings of guilt.

Mourning Your Hurt Self

When my father died suddenly in 1978, I denied his passing. When I overcame my denial, I was angry that he dared to leave me. After a while, I felt guilty about my anger and about everything I fantasized I could have done to make his life easier. Finally, I felt grief over the loss. Coming to grips with how you were impacted by your parents' co-dependency takes most of us along a similar path that uncovers the grief of loss only after many other feelings are experienced. This emotional trajectory is common—and healthy.

However, you may be surprised to discover that releasing your guilt has left you feeling quite sad. Your sadness is appropriate. Given your long-term pattern of denying a painful co-dependent history as well as suppressing a range of troublesome emotions, your commitment to recover is tantamount to killing off a significant portion of your psyche. You are legitimately mourning, then, the loss of your former unhealthy self.

There is an important difference though, between mourning and depression. When you are depressed you have lost control of your life; for long periods of time, you have no desire to function in the everyday world. The onset of depression is often inexplicable. Mourning, on the other hand, involves a *temporary* state of unhappiness that has a specific, identifiable origin. When you mourn, you are mourning the loss of something or somebody.

In the following exercises, allow yourself to mourn. You will be given techniques to acknowledge and nurture your hurt self, which will prepare you for the next stage of recovery.

Exercise: Keeping Quiet.   In his classic book, *Letters to a Young Poet,* German poet Rainer Maria Rilke wrote eloquent prose about the importance of keeping quiet, staying still, when we feel momentarily unhappy. According to Rilke, a short bout of sadness is no more than a temporary disequilibrium that should be tolerated quietly, with grace and nobility. Rilke insisted that we should not fight our discomfort, because there is always something to be learned from unhappiness.

To that end, this exercise asks that you take the time and find an appropriate place of solitude to mourn and to learn as much as you can about why you are mourning. Think. Cry. Express whatever you feel like expressing. Try not to struggle with your emotions, however. Give yourself the freedom to let go for a while. Remember, it's okay to feel sad about your childhood, about the quality of your relationship with your co-dependent parents. It's even okay to feel grief about giving up your emotional attachment to the feelings and behavioral patterns that have hurt you in the past.

Exercise: Your Journal as Confidante.   Margo, the adult daughter interviewed for the family profile in Chapter 4, The Critical Parent, permitted her journal to become her confidante when she began to mourn her past. As she wrote, she educated herself by exploring why she felt so unhappy; what she learned was that she needed to mourn and nurture the childhood memory she had of herself. That "little girl," she discovered, had impacted her adult life in unhealthy ways. As she wrote in her journal:

> I need to mourn for my little child that was brutalized by my parents....It is truly sad, gut-wrenching to picture this little girl who was in such need of love and who received instead hostile rejection. My little-girl-self was pure, wholly innocent, totally trusting, but because of the neuroses of her parents and the drama they were playing out, they couldn't give her what she craved—unconditional love. So she tried to please, tried to adapt and conform to

earn their love, but to no avail. So she felt lonely, isolated and alienated. She felt that everything was all her fault, so guilt also was a constant companion. Dread was ever-present as well—dread of their reaction to her, dread of punishment, dread of rejection.

How did I manage to survive? All my defense mechanisms kept me alive as an adult, but the quality of my life stank. The little girl in me still needed desperately to be loved, held, supported, encouraged, praised, valued, played with—basically, allowed to be her real self. But none of these things occurred because she got the message very early that she was not lovable, not worthwhile.

Now I can see just how precious, how special that little girl was (is). She deserves to be loved just for who she really is. The real miracle of life is that she is still within me, albeit she is encased in a lot of crap. But the crap can be slowly, deliberately stripped away. (This can be a painful process, too, because she's come to identify herself with a lot of this crap.) Yet, I know she's there, I can feel her; she makes me smile. *She is me and I am her.*

You, too, can gain insights about yourself and your family by using a journal or tape recorder to capture the memories and feelings that emerged from the quiet time you allowed yourself when working through the previous excerise.

Developing Compassion for Your Parents

Thus far, you have worked through exercises that have helped you to face harsh realities about the way you were raised. The exercises have also helped you cope with a range of emotions, from anger to guilt to grief. Basically, you have focused your recovery efforts on examining your parents' lives in terms of their co-dependency. To develop compassion for your parents, however, you will need to view them from a broader perspective to put their co-dependent behavior into context, to see your parents as multi-dimensional human beings.

For example, my own son was nearly an adult before I discovered that in some circles my mother was considered a saint of sorts because of the "miracles" she accomplished as principal of a high school that exclusively served children with disciplinary problems. Most of the parents of these young people had given up on their children and no longer expected them to complete high school. But my mother had different ideas about what these children could accomplish.

At 34, I decided to attend her school's graduation ceremony for the first time and was astonished by what I saw. There were tables and tables of entire families: mothers, fathers, aunts, uncles, all applauding and crying over their children having done the impossible—receiving a high school diploma. Virtually everyone present provided a testimonial about how none of this would have been possible without the intervention, patience, faith, and overall counseling skills of my mother.

Given the acrimonious relationship I had with my mother, it had simply never occurred to me that she was capable of such achievements. She and I had always related, as do most parents and children, in a very circumscribed and sometimes indirect manner. She was the critical parent; I was either the rebellious child thwarting her at every turn or the superachiever who secretly craved her approval. That graduation ceremony, however, proved also to be a graduation of sorts for me, because I began to see my mother in a different, more charitable light. From that day forward I could no longer see her solely as the ominous figure she had come to represent in my life.

You have already taken a first step in being able to view your parents with a more informed and compassionate eye by completing the exercises at the end of Chapter 7, The Ineffective Parent. Those exercises were designed to help you recognize the painful emotions that drive your parents' co-dependent behavior and your own symptoms of co-dependency. The exercise below will enable you to put your parents' co-dependent legacy into a broader and more compassionate framework by helping you learn more about their overall history. You will engage in activities that will answer such questions as: What do you know about your parents beyond the time they spent with you? What do you know about your parents' feelings? Their dreams? Hopes? Fears?

Exercise: Become Your Parents' Biographer.   Until recently, I knew very little about my mother's background; she had shared only a few stories about her past. My father had been a little more forthcoming, but not much. When I became a professional author and began to write profiles about people, it came as quite a shock to learn that, in some ways, I knew more about the lives of the people I interviewed than I knew about my own mother's and father's experiences. So I became my parents' biographer. What I discovered helped me to see them more clearly and more humanely, and I began to view them with compassion rather than with anger and scorn.

Deciding to assume the role of biographer is in some ways like donning a journalist's cap. You have the option of recording the data you collect either on paper or on a tape player. You will need to gather as much information as you can by using as many sources as possible. If your parents are alive, tell them you are interested in knowing more about their lives and ask if they will agree to an interview. Don't assume they'll be reluctant to talk to you, even if their co-dependent symptoms suggest a disinterest in sharing themselves with you. As children, even adult children, we tend to deal with our parents as if we are the center of the universe, as if their lives simply are not as important as ours. You may be surprised, therefore, at your parents' response to your genuine interest in them.

If your parents are dead, or they refuse to be interviewed, arrange to talk to other family members and your parents' professional colleagues and friends. Chapter 4's Margo, the adult daughter of a critical mother who has refused to acknowledge her daughter's existence for over 20 years, learned a lot about both of her parents by finding and talking to the doctor who treated her father for cancer.

This exercise will soon become an adventure, because you are almost guaranteed to be surprised by what you learn about your parents' past. One obvious benefit of this exercise is a deeper understanding of how your parents became the people they are today. Consequently, you will have created a wonderful opportunity for yourself—the chance to see your parents as whole people, multi-dimensional human beings who, like anyone else, deserve understanding and compassion.

If you still have difficulty making peace with your parents after completing this exercise, change the names in what you have written or taped, and then review the biography as if it were a story about two strangers. Can you feel concern or compassion for the key characters now?

PHASE TWO: MAKING PEACE WITH YOURSELF

You are your parents' child. They made some mistakes in the way they raised you, and you made some mistakes in the way you raised your own child. This phase will assist you in healing emotional wounds caused by your own co-dependent behavior. By working through the previous exercises, you have developed some valuable tools to help you view your parents and your relationship with them in a more healthy context. You will need to rely upon these tools to complete the exercises in the remaining phases of the recovery process.

Phase Two's exercises will help you do for yourself what you did for your parents in Phase One. You will confront your co-dependency, acknowledge your pain and guilt, mourn for having done what you said you would never do—make the same errors as your parents—and finally make peace with yourself by accepting and forgiving your imperfection.

Acknowledging Your Co-Dependency

It took me a long time to be able to admit that I was a co-dependent parent. It was very difficult for me to face my history of critical, demanding, disengaging parenting. I was upset by that discovery because of what it implied I had done to my only son. I was frustrated with myself as well because I had vowed that I would do a better job raising my son than my parents had with me. To discover that I had failed (by my impossible standards) was an unnerving realization. Identifying myself as a co-dependent was also troublesome for a less obvious reason: it violated the superachiever image I had worked so hard to cultivate.

All of the exercises in Chapters 3 through 7 were created to help you acknowledge whatever co-dependent patterns of behavior you have displayed over the years. Your recovery began the moment you were willing to recognize yourself as you turned the pages and read the descriptions of co-dependent parenting models. If you are not sure that your history of parenting warrants a "co-dependency" label, work through the exercises in this section anyway. You have nothing to lose. But you and your child have much to gain if, after further exploration, you determine that you are in fact co-dependent and that your initial uncertainty was due to denial.

Exercise: Joining a Support Group. To find out more about what it means to be a co-dependent parent, this exercise encourages you to join one or more support groups to help you identify and overcome your co-dependent symptoms. Some of these groups are for parents only, such as Parents Anonymous and Because I Love You, while others are open to any person suffering from co-dependency, such as Co-dependents Anonymous, Inc., commonly referred to as CODA. (For additional listings, see Appendix A at the back of this book.) Those groups that bill themselves as parent support groups are designed to help parents and their troubled children of all ages. Typically, such organizations meet weekly.

Virtually all of these organizations charge no dues or fees, and most follow the Twelve-Step program originated by Alcoholics Anonymous (AA). AA's Twelve-Step approach to recovery was adapted from a program begun by a group of men and women called the Oxford Movement. The members of the Oxford Movement were not alcoholics; they simply wanted a program that could help them live more satisfying lives. "Working" a Twelve-Step program involves the person-in-recovery (an addictive personality of some sort) undertaking a range of activities designed to maintain recovery. Some of the steps require that the person: acknowledge that a behavioral problem does in fact exist (in your case, co-dependency); take a long hard look at unhealthy behavioral patterns and the impact such patterns have had on others; admit to oneself and to others that mistakes have been made; and make amends, wherever possible, to whomever has been hurt by the unhealthy behavior.

One of the many benefits of joining a support group is that you will find that you are not alone, that there are many co-dependent parents in your community who are moving toward recovery. If you are having trouble acknowledging your co-dependent symptoms, you will find among such groups a supportive, caring environment that can help you confront your history of co-dependent parenting and begin to make real progress in changing your behavior.

Exercise: Becoming Aware of Repeat Performances. Another way of gaining insight into your own character is to examine the "bad" habits you've been unable to break. Make a list of such habits and honestly assess how you *and your child* are impacted by these addictive behavior patterns. For example, I had a habit of overcommitting myself in terms of my work. Every time I found myself panic-stricken for having scheduled enough work to take up a 24-hour day, I vowed never to do it again. Within weeks (sometimes days), however, I discovered I had backed myself up against the same wall again. When I candidly analyzed how my son was impacted by my behavior, it was easy to see that I was displaying classic co-dependent symptoms of disengaging parenting.

Exercise: Yourself, Your Parents. If you are still having difficulty identifying your own symptoms of co-dependency, consider the following: Were you able to acknowledge that your parents are co-dependent? If so, then by definition you, too, are a co-dependent because without exception, *co-dependent parents raise co-dependent children.*

Acknowledging Pain Caused by Your Co-Dependency

To admit that our behavior in any way has hurt our child has got to be one of the most difficult things for parents to do. We are afraid that we will be blamed by our child, afraid we'll be blamed by others, and afraid of the emotions this realization may evoke in our psyche. So our automatic tendency is to deny our co-dependent parenting behavior and its impact on our child. This tendency can be hard to overcome.

Ironically, when we find ourselves forced to cope with a son or daughter with behavioral problems, we often resort to scapegoating; we place the blame for our children's problems on our spouse, or some other circumstance or institution. A friend of mine, for example, holds the Army responsible for her son's becoming a heavy drinker. She conveniently overlooks the fact that her son used drugs prior to enlisting.

It is understandable that we as parents would want to avoid accepting some responsibility for our child's self-destructive behavior. But as long as we refuse to acknowledge the pain caused by our co-dependent legacy, we are doomed to perpetuate that legacy and are helpless to truly assist our child.

Exercise: Profiling Your Child.   One exercise to help you confront your feelings about the impact of your co-dependency on your child is to profile your son or daughter. First, make a list of your child's *most appealing* traits and habits. Think about how you have influenced your child to develop these good qualities. Next, list your child's *least appealing* traits and habits. Again, consider the role you played. If you are thwarted in this process and cannot make a connection between your actions and those of your child, ask yourself: Does it make sense to believe that you have the power to influence your child in positive ways, but no power to cause unhealthy behavior?

Exercise: Returning to Your Journal.   By now you are probably feeling the pain of facing the consequences of your co-dependent parenting. Even if you recognized yourself in the parenting models described in earlier chapters, examining how *your* behavior impacted *your* child may reverberate in ways more painful than merely recognizing yourself through the family profiles of others. Returning to your journal can help you release that pain. Write or record your feelings, and review what you have written or said.

Acknowledging your emotions, your thoughts, your beliefs through the use of a journal has a benefit beyond helping you to triumph over difficulties in your life. The more you use your journal, the more you are learning about your own value; in truth, you are treating yourself (via your journal) like a best friend.

Releasing Your Guilt

No matter what mistakes we make in raising our children, virtually all of us really do want the best for our offspring and are using every tool at our disposal to achieve that end. When we don't succeed, it's rarely because our intent was off the mark. Rather, we fail because our tools were inadequate, because our own co-dependent legacy interfered with our best intentions.

No wonder, then, we feel so much guilt when confronted with the knowledge that our co-dependency damaged our child. Most of us want to run and hide. Upon uncovering my own co-dependency, for example, I was reluctant to reveal myself to my son. For a while, my guilt was exacerbated by the realization that there was more to it than simply disappointment that my son had not achieved the noble goals I envisioned for him when he was a child. What also bothered me was that my image of myself had been tarnished—I had not turned out to be the wonderful mother I thought I would be.

Releasing my guilt, then, required that I acknowledge and learn how to deal with painful emotions generated by an awareness that my son was not the only victim of my co-dependency—I was a victim too. My recovery was tied to my son's recovery, as my son's was inextricably tied to mine. The exercise below will facilitate your recovery by helping you sort out what triggers your guilt and show you how to alter your behavior.

Exercise: Moral Codes Revisited. Like me, you probably have some definite ideas about what it means to be a "good" parent. The revelation of your co-dependency, though, has likely fouled your image of yourself as a perfect parent. If you are feeling acute guilt, it's because your belief system about what constitutes good parenting has been violated. So, to overcome your guilt for not achieving perfection in parenting, as well as for believing that you've failed your child, you will need to create a new set of moral codes that celebrates what it really means to be a parent and a human being.

First, you need to clearly determine your current belief system, the values that govern your life and comprise your moral codes. Complete this sentence: "I feel guilty because..." My response to this phrase was:

1. I feel guilty because, given my own dysfunctional upbringing, I should have known how to do a better job than my parents.

2. I feel guilty because parents are not supposed to fail their children as I failed my child.

3. I feel guilty because I should have been perfect.

These beliefs translate into moral codes that are disempowering because they reflect standards of behavior that are unattainable. Indeed, the standards I set up for myself permitted only one way for me to "win"—I had to deny my co-dependent symptoms and pretend that I was in fact a perfect parent. To do otherwise would have caused me to violate my moral codes and to feel guilty as a result. What I didn't understand until later was that following the dictates of my moral codes could only lead to a lose-lose outcome, because to "win" relied on my willingness to deny my real behavior and its results. A new set of moral codes that would encourage me to do a better job at parenting (rather than to hide my mistakes) would look like this:

1. I am not obligated to be a better parent than my parents.
2. It's okay that my child and I are not perfect.
3. I will continue to work hard at being the best parent I know how to be.

To develop a new set of moral codes, take yourself through the process outlined above. If you are still feeling guilty by acknowledging your co-dependency, its impact on your child, and your damaged self-image, examine your new list of moral codes to see whether you have violated *those* values or your *old* value system. If you are still clinging to your old set of moral codes, candidly consider why you want to feel bad about yourself. What need are you feeding? Do you still aspire to be perfect?

Mourning Your Mistakes

Your guilt, once released, is likely to be replaced with feelings of sadness. Basically, you will be mourning your decision to recover and thus give up a lifelong attachment to your unhealthy history—your belief in your would-be perfection and the co-dependent behavior you developed to compensate for your imperfection. In addition, grieving over your own human inadequacy is likely to stir feelings of grief about your parents' mistakes, since your co-dependent legacy is closely woven into that of your parents.

To overcome such emotions, you will need to allow yourself to express what you feel: rage, grief, sadness, whatever comes up. The bottom line is that you don't attempt to suppress or deny the painful feelings that are bound to emerge.

Exercise: Understanding More About the Nature of Your Grief. For those of you who still question the value of mourning, I especially recommend that you read Alice Miller's *The Drama of the Gifted Child: The Search for the True Self*, and John Bradshaw's book *Bradshaw On: The Family*. Both are listed in Appendix B: References and Suggested Reading. By taking the time to read these two books you will better understand why I have included grieving in your recovery process. Miller writes that the payoff for your willingness to mourn is the "achievement of freedom." Bradshaw agrees: "Mourning is the only way to heal the hole in the cup of our soul."

Exercise: Again, Your Journal. It is particularly useful to return to your journal during your period of grief. Write or tape your thoughts, feelings, actions, choices. Consider your journal a nurturing tool. You are, after all, becoming your own witness, which is a powerful form of validation.

Developing Compassion for Yourself

Phase Two of your recovery process has covered much of the same ground you explored in Phase One: Making Peace with Your Parents, but with a decidedly different twist—the parent in question this time is you. For that reason, it may have been more difficult territory to travel emotionally. The upside, however, is that what you were eventually able to do for your parents—develop compassion, and perhaps even forgive the effects of their co-dependency—you can also do for yourself.

The following exercise helps you place your co-dependent past in a more healthy context. Chapter 7's exercises represented an attempt to start this process; there you were asked to identify the underlying emotions associated with your and your parents' co-dependent symptoms. I hope that you began to see just how human we all are, that even the most-difficult-to-deal-with behavior typically masks feelings such as fear, desperation, insecurity, and shame.

Exercise: Become Your Own Biographer. Sometimes it's easier to generate feelings of compassion for others than for ourselves. To illustrate, I have always been my own worst critic. I often gave my friends much more room to stumble than I gave myself. For this exercise, then, write or tape your own biography, but use a different name than your own. The purpose of this substitution is to distance yourself from what you are reading about yourself.

Be as thorough in researching this exercise as you were in developing your parents' biography. Interview your sisters, brothers, aunts, uncles, parents, and, if you are very brave, your own children. If you have a best friend, talk to him or her as well. Brace yourself for this exercise, because you may be surprised by what you learn. It's important to be as dispassionate as possible during the "data collection." Try not to show any emotion as you listen to what your interviewees have to say. Where appropriate, ask them about their memories of you as a baby, as an adolescent, as an adult.

When you have completed this project, read or listen to what you have prepared as if it were about someone else. Are there moments when you are moved to cry? To laugh? Is this the story of a complete person who has experienced sorrow, pain, confusion, and happiness? Now compare what you have written about yourself to the biography you developed for your parents. Are there similarities? Is it possible now to feel for yourself what you felt upon reading your parents' story—compassion?

PHASE THREE: MAKING PEACE WITH YOUR CHILD

By now you are prepared and have the tools to do what is for most parents the inconceivable: confront your child with your mistakes, your shortcomings, your sorrow. Such extraordinary acts will be requested of you in Phase Three so that you may accomplish the extraordinary: to free yourself by freeing your child, through the act of reaching out to include your child in your recovery process. In this way you will have taken a large step toward breaking the cycle of co-dependency that has plagued your family generation after generation.

Indeed, you will have graced yourself with some measure of freedom, because you and your child will not be as locked into the "co" part of the co-dependent game. In the past, when playing that game, the two of you were unconsciously required to behave in a way that maintained each other's neediness and low self-esteem. By making peace with your child, both you and your offspring will be free to act differently, to discover who you really are. In addition, your child will have been exposed to a recovery process that will serve her well for many years to come. This includes the provision—if the need arises—of tools to reach out similarly to her own child one day.

The exercises in Phase Three can contribute to the overall well-being of a child of any age. Whether your children are adolescents or adults, they will directly benefit by participating with you in the exercises. Even if your children are preadolescent, do not skip Phase Three; what is discussed, along with the exercises, will provide you with valuable tools and techniques you may use at a later date.

Helping Your Child Acknowledge Your Co-Dependency

Just as it may have been hard for you to acknowledge your parents' co-dependency, it's likely that your child is having difficulty facing the fact that you are less than perfect. If your co-dependent parenting has taken the form of the mythic hero syndrome, for instance, your child will be particularly reluctant to accept your imperfection.

Moreover, for most children, the decision to communicate feelings or thoughts about their parents *to* their parents is a grave decision, because of what they believe is at stake: the loss of their parents' love. Also, a common symptom found in virtually all co-dependent families is the admonition to keep secrets. So it's not surprising that your child may avoid being open and honest about your co-dependency.

Nevertheless, you need to help your child acknowledge, understand, and accept what you have learned about yourself: that you are a co-dependent parent who has made mistakes along the way. The exercises below can help you become a more healthy role model. Indeed, the most powerful and therapeutic tool you can give your child to overcome a co-dependent legacy is to behave in a way that vividly demonstrates the emphasis you place on speaking and living honestly.

Exercises: Establishing a Dialogue.   Here you will encourage your child to participate in a number of exercises that expand on some of the earlier chapters and on Phases One and Two of the Four-Phase Healing Program. Before your child begins these new exercises, explain how you are trying to become both a better parent and person and will need your child's help to accomplish such goals. Tell your child that you want her to work through some exercises that will assist you in seeing yourself through your child's eyes.

Depending upon the age of your child, you should decide which of the exercises below to share with your child. Allow as much time as necessary for these discussions. Explain to your child that you genuinely want her honest appraisal of your past behavior and that there will be no punishment or blame for telling the truth, no matter what is said. Then prepare yourself to make good your promise as you coach your child into completing the following activities:

1. Share with your child the list of "bad" habits you have been unable to break and your assessment of how such habits have impacted your child, as described in Phase Two's Becoming Aware of Repeat Performances exercise. Find out if your child agrees or disagrees. Get your child to tell you how she feels about your bad habits; ask if she can identify some patterns of behavior you've overlooked. Your child probably will be hesitant to open up at first, but persist. Most children want the opportunity to talk, to give their opinion.

2. Show your child the list of family secrets from your childhood that you compiled for the Exposing Family Secrets exercise in Phase One. Ask your child if she can make or recite a similar list about the immediate family, and then discuss your child's findings. Explain how you now want to bring the family secrets out into the open. Ask your child's advice as to the best way to reveal the family secrets. For example, who should know about the substance abuse of a sibling?

3. Tell your child about the exercise you finished in Chapter 3, in which you examined how you handled your own child around three areas of struggle that created conflict between you and your parents when you were growing up. Once you have shared your view of the problems you and your child are having, solicit the child's opinion. Try to establish a dialogue, especially if your version of events differs from hers. Explain that you learned from your parents some of the behavior you are trying to alter, and that you want to help your child to avoid developing some of the same behavior.

Helping Your Child Acknowledge Pain

When you help your child overcome his resistance to accepting your co-dependency, he will likely respond emotionally to what you've told him. But he may not explicitly demonstrate his pain. The anger, shame, or angst may go unexpressed. Often, children are afraid of experiencing and displaying harsh or "negative" feelings toward their parents. They are particularly afraid of reprisals and the ultimate punishment: a withdrawal of the parents' love.

However, just as it was unhealthy for you to choke off your emotions, as discussed in the prior two phases, your child will suffer as well unless you actively help him express and cope with such feelings.

Exercises: Parents as Compassionate Witnesses.   Years ago, when my son was 13, I noticed he was very angry with me, he took sarcastic swipes at every opportunity. Finally, I approached him and asked if he wanted to tell me what was wrong, to speak candidly without fear of punishment. At first he didn't quite believe my offer. But once he warmed up, he recounted every infraction, every poor decision I had made about his upbringing from the time he was 4 years old. No doubt this exchange (I mostly listened) was more painful for me than for him. I had to apologize more than once. However, he and our relationship benefited immensely from what became a three-hour discussion; it established a pattern of communication that prevails to this day. My son is now comfortable sharing many types of experiences and feelings with me, including the first time he experimented with marijuana and with sex.

These exercises will ask you to become your child's best friend, a compassionate witness. Take ample time to set up each of the exercises below, and then listen intently and with compassion to your child express a range of emotions, some of which may prove unpleasant for you. Handle what you hear with as much aplomb and dignity as possible: Remember, this is a cathartic and therefore healthy experience for your child.

1. Share with your child the exercise you completed at the end of Chapter 4, in which you listed at least five pivotal incidents from your childhood. You also developed a similar list of what you believed your child would consider the most significant incidents from her past that involved you. Ask your child if she agrees with your assessment. If not, try to get her to tell you why.

2. Let your child know that you worked through an exercise in Chapter 5 that asked you to explain why you were motivated to perform at least five activities for her that you really did not believe would serve her best interest. Ask your child if she agrees with your conclusions. If not, get her to tell you her reasons.

Exercise: Just Say, "I'm Sorry."   This exercise makes only one request of you: be willing to tell your child you're sorry for the mistakes you now recognize you made. Jan, the daughter of the critical mother who was quoted in the Phase One exercises, underscores the importance of a parent's ability to show that type of strength and courage: "I only wanted to hear acknowledgment [of her mother's co-dependent parenting]; just once I wanted my mother to break down and cry and say she was sorry. Had she done that, I could have more easily put my life back together."

Helping Your Child Release Guilt

Just as you were uncomfortable venting anger, resentment, and frustration toward your parents, you should anticipate that your child may feel a similar reluctance. So once your child has released pent-up emotions, you may need to help him overcome guilt. Again, guilt is associated with the violation of a person's values, which are reflected by the underlying moral codes.

A child's values are, not surprisingly, connected to the co-dependent behavior of the parents. If, for example, the child has been made to feel insecure by a demanding parent about whether or not he is loved, the child will be even more prone to guilt feelings upon completing the exercises described in the previous section. The following exercise will focus on what a parent can do to help a child cope with guilt provoked by the emotional pain of recognition that his parents truly are not perfect.

Exercise: Express Your Love.   This exercise is simple, but it may be very difficult. In my family, we rarely verbally expressed our love. Consequently, at least two of us three children questioned our mother's love. All you need to do in this exercise is assure your child that you love her—and make sure you use those words. Say, "I love you, so there is no need to feel guilty." Let your child know that your love for her was never at stake. Such unequivocal statements will help your child begin to live by a moral code that states: A child can be angry at her parents and still express love and be loved by her mother and father. Expressions of love and anger are not mutually exclusive; one does not invalidate the other.

Helping Your Child Mourn

Now that your child understands that she does not have to feel guilty when she expresses authentic emotion and, therefore, does not have to repress her pain, she will probably experience some sadness. Essentially, she will be mourning the loss of a co-dependent symptom that was key to her survival.

Your child may feel as if the rug has been snatched out from under her. By initiating a recovery process that involves her participation, you are changing the rules of the game the two of you have played for many years. By now, *you* know that to mourn a loss of any kind is healthy, but your child may be confused by what she is feeling. Your patience, awareness, and wisdom will be needed to guide your child through this step of the recovery process.

Exercise: I'm Okay, You're Okay.   This exercise asks that you reassure your child that experiencing feelings of confusion and grief is okay. Beyond that, reassure him that *he* is okay. Share with your child what you have learned about loss and mourning. Emphasize the fact that feeling grief is a healthy, normal experience, and that you went through the same process. Invite your child to ask questions about what you felt and what he is feeling. Above all, let your child know that you love and understand him, and that you will be there to help him sort out his confusion, grief, and fear.

Exercise: Journal—An Introduction.   Introduce your child to the value of using a journal as a way of expressing her feelings and thoughts. Give her an exercise that requires her to experiment with the use of her journal. Ask her to record (via the written word or tape player), without holding back, how mourning is affecting her. Then invite her to examine what she has written or said with the understanding that the grieving process always provides an opportunity to learn something about oneself. Suggest that she make a list of her findings. Share with her at least one insight you gained from your experience with mourning; ask her to share with you the results of her exercise.

Helping Your Child Develop Compassion

Overall, the exercises in Phase Three have encouraged you to show your child compassion; to recognize, support, and celebrate your child's multi-dimensionality. What may not be as clear, however, is that you have gained as much as you have given from your willingness to participate in these exercises. This is true because your child can now see you in a broader, more human context. You have already increased your child's capacity to feel compassion toward you and your co-dependency, toward his own imperfect self, and toward the world at large.

The remaining exercises for this phase will add one more facet to the work you and your child have already accomplished: your child will explore with you the emotions that drive your co-dependent parenting, and your child will be provided with a historical backdrop—he will learn more about the person you were before you became a parent.

Exercise: Revealing Your Humanness.   Show your child the chart you prepared for Chapter 7 that displayed what you were really feeling when your behavior was difficult for your child to deal with. Is your child surprised to discover you sometimes feel fear, anxiety, or sadness, as he does? Generate a discussion about why you feel the way you do. Help your child see the similarities between what provokes an emotional reaction in you and in your child. Make sure that you talk about the fact that you are human, too.

Exercise: Revealing Your Past.   Let your child read or listen to the biographies you prepared for your parents and for yourself, during exercises in Phases One and Two. Share with your child what you learned about yourself and your parents. Tell your child how your perceptions of your own life and that of your parents changed, and how the new perceptions enriched your life and why. Be prepared to answer questions. Suggest that your child undertake a similar project and later share it with you. Encourage her to interview others, including you.

PHASE FOUR: THE VALIDATING PARENT

Thus far, you have been asked to acknowledge long-standing patterns of co-dependency in yourself and in your parents, and to learn how to cope with that awareness. You also have been given general guidelines for establishing new patterns of behavior through the open and honest dialogues you had with yourself and your child.

This final phase of the Four-Phase Healing Program will teach you how you can become a validating parent. The validating parent model will be described; exercises will be provided to help you develop and reinforce new and more healthy patterns of behavior; and you will be exposed to a new way of speaking that will reflect a confidence-enhancing parenting model, rather than the confidence-diminishing perspective that supported your co-dependency.

"You're a Good Person, I Like You"

You were exhibiting some of the traits of a validating parent when you completed the exercises that required you to be honest with yourself and your child. You were behaving like a validating parent when you demonstrated self-confidence by allowing yourself to be vulnerable, to trust that your child would not use what he was learning against you.

Validating parents are mothers and fathers who routinely display the traits you are developing. As a result, they raise healthy, confident, responsible children capable of handling themselves in the "real" world, because these young people genuinely like themselves. They like themselves because they have the strength of character to tell the truth about what they feel and believe, and therefore to expose their real selves. In other words, such children are a reflection of their validating parents. Basically, these parents have given their daughters and sons the message, "You're a good person, I like you," despite their children's mistakes and human imperfection.

New Language to Live By

One practical technique validating parents employ to help their children feel good about themselves is to communicate by using clear, supportive, and empowering language, unlike the messages delivered by their co-dependent counterparts. To get an idea of what this means, I have selected the following statements from a list developed by teachers of effective parenting from the Hacienda–La Puente School District:

- "I really liked the way you did that."
- "That shows you put a lot of work into it."
- "I know it must be disappointing, because I know you really tried."
- "I'm so proud of you."
- "You did that so well. Show me how to do it."
- "You really are a great help."
- "Did I ever tell you how much I love you?"
- "I really respect your opinion."

Basically, this is the language of a parent who truly respects and loves her child. The validating parent, then, *validates the best in her child.* Exercises in the next section will help you develop this characteristic.

Healthy Family Life–Three Key Factors

Your recovery from a history of co-dependent parenting will have a crucial impact on other family members, particularly your child. Thus, you should expect your family dynamic to change–perhaps drastically. There is no generic description for how your more healthy family will relate, though, or specifically how each family member will behave.

Researchers have found that there are a number of key factors typically present in most effectively run households. With that knowledge, you can develop new patterns of behavior to build into your daily family life. Three of the most important of these factors are:

1. Clear communication.
2. Validation of feelings and beliefs.
3. Respect for individuality.

These factors are adapted from *Essentials of a Healthy Family: Family Factors* by family specialist, Dr. Donald Cadagon.

Exercise: Clear and Honest Communication. Your recovery in part will depend on your willingness to overcome a prevalent habit of co-dependent parents: the tendency to communicate unclear, untrue, and invalidating messages that accuse or blame your child. This exercise will ask you to create a new way of speaking to your child by understanding the value and mastering the use of direct "I" messages. A direct "I" message is a statement that you claim responsibility for and ownership of. Examples include:

- "I am confused about why you behaved that way."
- "I am really pleased by this report card."
- "I am saddened by what I've just heard."

Benefits of this way of talking are numerous. First, by claiming ownership, you relate honesty and openness. "I" messages also communicate to your child exactly what the impact of her behavior has been, rather than leaving that determination to the child's imagination. It is less threatening for a child to hear you simply state what you feel—no matter what the emotion—than to be accused of *causing* your feelings. To that end, "I" messages deal directly with your child's offending behavior as distinct from your child's character or personal value. Consequently, the child's self-esteem is not in question.

"I" messages imply that you trust and respect your child, because you are demonstrating confidence in your child's willingness to modify behavior that works against his own well-being as well as others. Such direct messages also help a child discover the boundaries of what is and what is not acceptable behavior.

Exercise: Validation of Feelings and Beliefs. Parents who validate the feelings and beliefs of their children allow their offspring the right to feel and believe whatever they feel and believe, even when such emotions and opinions differ from those of their parents. Moreover, children who are raised by validating parents are encouraged to express their emotions and opinions at the first appropriate opportunity. By so doing, there is little chance for any pent-up emotion or damaging misunderstanding to get suppressed or go unnoticed or unclarified. Such an environment also permits positive emotions, experiences, and behaviors to get quickly validated, which is a real morale booster and builds high self-esteem.

To validate your child's feelings and beliefs, you are asked in this exercise to establish a Family Town Hall that meets on a regular basis, similar to the Feelings Round adopted by the family profiled in Chapter 3, The Demanding Parent. Your Town Hall should begin by providing every family member with the opportunity to report what is on his or her mind. Judgments should be disallowed; comments should be withheld until everyone has had a turn to speak.

If your children are babies, start doing this exercise with your spouse or significant other, so that your child will be exposed to the activity at an early age. As you acquire practice in this technique, the relationship between you and your partner will surely improve in the long run. If your children are adults and have moved away from home, implement some version of this exercise by designating a certain time each week or month when you telephone your offspring for this purpose.

Exercise: Respect for Individuality.   Validating parents demonstrate a respect for their child's individuality by resolving differences between the child and the parent through negotiation instead of by co-dependent solutions such as demanding total acquiescence or "compromise" without the child's participation. The validating parenting model accepts that a legitimate difference exists. The parent then seeks to resolve conflicts by placing an emphasis on compatible desires or shared goals, rather than on differences.

This exercise asks that you use your Family Town Hall to help your child develop individual goals as well as engage your child's participation in the development of group goals for the family. When problems inevitably arise, use the forum provided by the Family Town Hall to negotiate a solution that is compatible with clearly stated individual and group goals, priorities, and concerns. One significant advantage of this approach is that since all of the members of your family will have shared in the development of each other's and the family's goals, they will have a vested interest in seeing to it that problems are resolved to the benefit of everyone as much as possible.

By choosing to head a healthy family, you have embarked upon a most noble undertaking. By reading this book and working through all of the exercises, you have begun a process of recovery that will break your legacy of co-dependent parenting and therefore alter your life, the lives of your children, and the lives of many generations to come. And though your recovery task will at times be frustrating and painful, have faith. Your decision will lead you down an often rocky, but an always rewarding, road.

EPILOGUE

Always when I write, I am changed by the experience. This time, I learned from my own commentary in Chapter 9: "You will need periodically to repeat or review the exercises that comprise the four-phase healing process." I decided to take my own advice while completing this book. I worked through some of the Phase One exercises and discovered, to my surprise, that I had not quite made peace with my mother. Consequently, I had yet to make peace with myself and with my son.

I had gotten stuck in my recovery process because of the skewed way in which I was examining my mother's history. Though I recognized that she was a multi-dimensional person, her good qualities still paled in my memory. Instead, I chose to remember vividly her co-dependent past and therefore focused on her shortcomings rather than her strengths. Basically, I was still clinging to my anger about the way I was raised.

As I worked through "Developing Compassion for Your Parents" in Chapter 9, I followed my own instructions and reexamined the exercise I had completed at the end of Chapter 7. That exercise asked readers to identify the painful emotions that drive the co-dependent behavior in their parents and in themselves. Upon reviewing that work, I realized that my mother and I had much in common. That realization caused me to think about how similar our personalities were—in both our appealing and unappealing traits. After some thought, I came to this conclusion: I really like my mother, *and* myself. In fact, I was struck at that moment by how much I love my mother.

With that insight, I felt a burden had been lifted from my shoulders. For many years I had silently believed that I wasn't okay, that I needed to alter myself in some significant way to meet my own unattainable standards. So it was exhilarating to accept that Mom was okay and, given that I am my mother's child, that I am okay as well.

It took me a couple of days, though, to muster up the nerve to call my mother to share my revelation. When I did, my greeting was: "Hi, Mom. I just called to tell you that I love you. I have no other purpose than that." Those words opened up a floodgate of emotions for both of us, and began my recovery process anew.

What I learned from that experience was this: My reluctance to accept my mother's fine qualities impaired my ability to accept that I, too, had equally fine qualities. And what I had a difficult time accepting about myself, I had a hard time accepting about my son. Specifically, I had grown impatient with his difficulty with growing up, the mistakes he was making on his way to becoming a man. My hard-won awareness, then, helped me finally to make peace with my mother, myself, and my son.

SELF-HELP AND SUPPORT GROUPS FOR CO-DEPENDENT PARENTS AND THEIR FAMILIES

Al-Anon Family Group Headquarters
1372 Broadway
New York, NY 10018
(212) 302-7240

Al-Anon provides support services for people related to alcoholics or who have friends with alcohol problems. Alateen, connected to Al-Anon, is a support group for young people ages 12–20 with drinking problems. Lay therapy groups are free and can be very helpful.

Alcoholics Anonymous World Services
P.O. Box 459, Grand Central Station
New York, NY 10163
(212) 686-1100

Alcoholics Anonymous meetings consist of people sharing their experience, strength, and hope with other members of the group. Some meetings also feature guest lectures. All programs are anonymous; no last names are used. AA provides a beneficial, safe place to discuss your problems and gain support and encouragement from others like you. The organization has assisted millions of people in leading productive, sober lives.

Because I Love You
P.O. Box 67065
Los Angeles, CA 90067-0006
(213) 659-5289
(818) 882-4881

This Southern California–based organization is a parent-support group designed to help parents who have children of any age with behavioral problems, such as substance abuse, physical or verbal abuse, defiance of authority, irregular school attendance, or running away from home.

Co-Dependents Anonymous, Inc.

P.O. Box 33577
Phoenix, AZ 85067-3577
(602) 277-7991

Often referred to as CODA, this international organization is for people 16 years old and over whose common problem is an inability to maintain functional, healthy relationships with their mates, their children, other family members, friends, and co-workers. CODA is a 12-step program.

Childhelp USA

6463 Independence Avenue
Woodland Hills, CA 91367
(800) 4-A-CHILD
(818) 347-7280

For people feeling overwhelmed by parental responsibilities, Childhelp USA offers a professional counselor who will offer advice and referrals to local groups and organizations that can provide assistance. They also run the Village of Childhelp, a residential treatment center for severely abused and neglected children ages 2–12.

Families Anonymous

P.O. Box 528
Van Nuys, CA 91408
(800) 736-9805 (24-hour information line)
(818) 989-7841

Families Anonymous is an organization whose structure is similar to AA: a self-help program for families and friends of drug abusers, with no dues or fees for participants; personal anonymity is preserved and no appointment is necessary. FA has groups throughout the United States and in Canada, and is expanding overseas as well.

National Association for Adult Children of Dysfunctional Families

842 Forest Circle
Fond du Lac, WI 54935
(414) 921-6991

Primarily a referral agency to help adult children of dysfunctional families reduce shame, guilt, and compulsive behavior, NAACDF provides resources and information about support groups in geographic locations nationwide.

Parents Anonymous
22330 Hawthorne Blvd., Suite 208
Torrance, CA 90505
(800) 352-0386 (24-hour hotline, California)
(800) 421-0353 (USA, outside California)

For parents who have abused a child, for the spouse of such a parent, or for a victim of abuse who needs parenting skills, Parents Anonymous can offer help. It offers member-led as well as therapist-led counseling groups, and provides a 24-hour hotline to call if you are becoming abusive with your child and need immediate counseling. PA has offices throughout the United States, Canada, England, and Germany.

Parents Involved Network
311 So. Juniper Street, Suite 902
Philadelphia, PA 19107
(215) 735-2465

Parents Involved Network enables parents to share common concerns, exchange information, and influence programs and policy issues that affect the treatment, education, and service needs of children and adolescents with emotional problems. PIN is sponsored by the Mental Health Association of Southeastern Pennsylvania.

Parents United
(Daughters United/Sons United)
P.O. Box 952
San Jose, CA 95108
(408) 280-5055
(408) 279-8228 (crisis line)

Parents United provides support for families in which incest has occurred. This support includes weekly professional counseling, lay therapy groups, and long-term support where incest has been a factor in family difficulty. PU also offers to arrange for medical, vocational, and legal counseling.

Secular Organization for Sobriety
Box 15781
North Hollywood, CA 91615
(818) 980-8851
(213) 302-7240
   If the spiritual component of AA is unappealing to you, you may contact SOS, an organization of similar goals and structure.

T.A.L.K. for Parents
Shadow Mountain High School
2902 E. Shea Blvd.
Phoenix, AZ 85028
(602) 953-2610
   A support group for mothers and fathers whose children are exhibiting behavioral problems.

ToughLove
P.O. Box 1069
Doylestown, PA 18901
(215) 348-7090 (Pennsylvania)
(818) 843-5689 (California)
   A national support group for parents with difficult-to-manage children, ToughLove helps parents set guidelines and rules for behavior in the home, and trains parents in how to enforce those rules.

Wisconsin Family Ties
P.O. Box 56064
Madison, WI 53705
(800) 362-3020
(608) 267-6888
   Wisconsin Family Ties is a statewide network of local support groups composed of parents whose children have emotional or behavioral disabilities. WFT offers support, education, and training for parents and also provides assistance to existing parent-support groups.

REFERENCES AND SUGGESTED READING

Beattie, Melody. *Codependent No More: How to Stop Controlling Others and Start Caring for Yourself.* San Francisco: Harper & Row, 1987.

Becnel, Barbara Cottman. *Parents Who Help Their Children Overcome Drugs.* Los Angeles: Lowell House, 1989.

Black, Claudia. *Children of Alcoholics: As Youngsters-Adolescents-Adults.* New York: Ballantine Books, 1981.

Bradshaw, John. *Bradshaw On: The Family.* Deerfield Beach, Florida: Health Communications, Inc., 1988.

Cadagon, Donald. *Essentials of a Healthy Family: Family Factors.* A handout used by the Hacienda–La Puente School District for effective parenting class.

Casey, James. *The History of the Family: New Perspectives on the Past.* Oxford, England: Basil Blackwell Inc., 1989.

Co-Dependency: An Emerging Issue. Pompano Beach, Florida: Health Communications, Inc., 1984.

Engel, Beverly. *Divorcing a Parent: Free Yourself from the Past and Live the Life You've Always Wanted.* Los Angeles: Lowell House, 1990.

Erickson, Gerald D., and Terrence P. Hogan. *Family Therapy: An Introduction to Theory and Technique.* Monterey, California: Brooks/Cole Publishing Company, 1981.

Farmer, Steven. *Adult Children of Abusive Parents.* Los Angeles: Lowell House, 1989.

Forward, Dr. Susan, with Craig Buck. *Toxic Parents: Overcoming Their Hurtful Legacy and Reclaiming Your Life.* New York: Bantam Books, 1989.

Freeman, Lucy, and Herbert S. Stream. *Guilt: Letting Go.* New York: John Wiley & Sons, 1986.

Gurman, Alan S., and David P. Kniskern. *Handbook of Family Therapy.* New York: Brunner/Mazel, 1981.

Haley, Jay. *Uncommon Therapy: The Psychiatric Techniques of Milton H. Erickson, M.D.* New York: W. W. Norton & Company, 1973.

James, John W., and Frank Cherry. *The Grief Recovery Handbook: A Step-By-Step Program for Moving Beyond Loss.* New York: Harper & Row, 1988.

Leonard, Linda Schierse. *The Wounded Woman: Healing the Father-Daughter Relationship.* New York: Shambhala Publications, 1985.

Miller, Alice. *The Drama of the Gifted Child: The Search for the True Self.* New York: Basic Books, Inc., 1981.

Rogers, Ronald L., Chandler Scott McMillin, and Morris A. Hill. *The Twelve Steps Revisited.* New York: Bantam Books, 1990.

INDEX